MOTIVATION FROM THE HEART

The Guide to Motivational Leadership

By Richard Tiller and Paul Renker

© 2007 Richard Tiller, Paul Renker
all rights reserved.

ISBN 0-9630722-1-8

Printed in the U.S.A. by Tiller Marketing Services,
www.richardtiller.com

Table Of Contents

PART ONE DEFINING MOTIVATION

Chapter 1 What Is Motivation? 7
Chapter 2 Motivational Leadership 13

PART TWO CREATING AN ENVIRONMENT FOR MOTIVATION

Chapter 3 Belief...29
Chapter 4 Energy 51
Chapter 5 Creating an Environment of Joy 71
Chapter 6 Motivation with High Standards 91
Chapter 7 Direction and Empowerment 135

PART THREE TEACHING ATTITUDES FOR SUCCESS

Chapter 8 Building Your Team's Self-Confidence 149
Chapter 9 Teaching Relaxed Focus......................................181
Chapter 10 Teaching Mental Toughness............................205

Part One

DEFINING MOTIVATION

CHAPTER 1

WHAT IS MOTIVATION?

Who is the most motivated person you can imagine?

What is it about him or her that personifies motivation to you?

You are now thinking of someone who demonstrates motivation in a way that inspires others – a role model for motivation in its highest form. What is it about such people that earns them admirable distinction? What is it that motivates them? Are they afraid of their boss? Are they afraid of punishment or failure? Is it only about the money? Or does their motivation have deeper roots?

Do they seem motivated only by short-term goals and rewards, or do they seem equally motivated over the longer term? Are they more motivated by external forces, or does their motivation come mostly from within? Are they motivated primarily by others, or are they self-motivated?

To have earned your respect as someone who epitomizes motivation to you, they probably embody three characteristics:

1. A strong belief in themselves.
2. A strong belief in their purpose.
3. A strong desire to improve every day.

Now suppose that as a leader your desire is to help those you lead to develop the kind of motivation your role model radiates? How would you do it? The answer to that question is the subject of this book.

A frequently debated question about motivation is whether you can truly motivate other people on a deep and meaningful level. We know we can create short-term motivation through reward and punishment. But what about deeper, long-term motivation? Can that be instilled by someone else, or does it come only from within? Is true motivation a rare gift reserved only for a chosen few, or can it be inspired in anyone? How much difference can a leader really make?

As a leader you can have a huge impact on the motivation of your followers. Motivation is one of your most meaningful responsibilities and lasting contributions and may ultimately be the most valuable legacy of your leadership.

When people have a strong belief in themselves and in their purpose, they are more motivated. This motivation stimulates the desire to keep improving. The kind of belief we are talking about here is an internal motivation. It is so important that we will spend Chapter Three delving deeper into it. You cannot provide internal motivation. You provide external motivation. How does this help? Because your external motivation increases their internal motivation by enhancing their belief in themselves and their purpose. This belief in self and purpose makes them want to keep improving. When you see people who want to keep improving, you know they are motivated at the deepest level.

The stronger our internal motivation, the more receptive we are to external motivation. The stronger external motivation you provide, the more the internal motivation of your followers can flourish.

Great leaders provide both short-term and long-term motivation. Short-term motivation is valuable. It helps us fulfill short-term goals. Sometimes reward versus punishment is all it takes to create short-term motivation.

However, this book is about long-term motivation. Long-term motivation requires belief in yourself and in your purpose, and a desire to improve every day.

One reason for motivating others is to achieve goals, but deeper motivation is much more valuable. The higher purpose of motivating others is to help them fulfill their potential and maximize their opportunities. Often you will even inspire them to exceed their expectations of themselves, and to achieve more than they ever thought possible.

Most people don't really want to be excellent at what they do. They want to be acceptable. They may say they want to be excellent, but they're not willing to do what it takes. They don't see the point in it. It's not worth the effort to them. They don't have enough belief in themselves or their purpose to want to improve every day until they become excellent, and then still keep improving. This is a drive which distinguishes champions from everyone else. Champions want to be the best, and then they still want to get better. They believe in themselves and in their purpose so much that they are unstoppable.

This is where you really can make a difference as a leader. You can enhance your followers' belief in themselves and their purpose so that they want to be excellent at what they do, and they want to keep getting better. Eventually this desire creates a momentum of its own. But you can get it started, and you can help them keep it going.

How do people feel when they are truly motivated at a profound level? We have already said they believe in themselves and their purpose. They feel as though they are achieving something of value, something meaningful. They feel recognized, appreciated, valued, and wanted for who they are and for what they have achieved. They feel a high sense of self-worth and self-confidence.

Motivation at its most profound level also produces other feelings which help us achieve great things. When we feel genuinely motivated we can feel some or all of the following:

- Confident
- Fearless
- Energized
- Empowered
- Passionate
- Focused
- Competitive
- Hopeful
- Respected
- Trusted
- Joyful

So in this book we are talking about motivating on a deeper level than merely to excite, stimulate, urge or coerce. We are talking about motivating people to perform at their highest level by increasing their belief in themselves and in their purpose. We are talking about inspiring, uplifting, energizing and empowering them. Enabling them to raise their own standards for themselves. Improving self-image, expanding self-definition, destroying their self-limiting self-definitions.

We have to accept the reality that motivation comes primarily from within. Some people are more naturally motivated than others. All other things being equal, they will be more successful. Also, people are motivated in different ways at different times to do different things. In other words, motivation is a moving target. Most of the time, we will be more successful in those endeavors where we feel more motivated.

Tony Robbins writes, *"The greatest gift that extraordinarily successful people have over the average person is their ability to get themselves to take action"* (Robbins 1986, p. 7). So where does that leave leaders who are trying to motivate their followers? It means that your ultimate goal as a motivator is not merely to motivate other people, but also to teach them how to motivate themselves. You can influence what they feel most motivated to achieve. Yet you have to accept the fact that every person is ultimately responsible for their own motivation, and that there are many other factors in their lives influencing the direction and level of their motivation. While you may not be able to single-handedly shape the direction or level of their motivation, you can certainly provide a profound positive influence, and you can have an important effect on the level of success they achieve. You can make a huge difference, and this book will show you how to do it.

The goal of this book extends beyond explaining how to motivate those you lead. It is to define a leadership mindset – a total way of thinking – that is focused on motivation every day. This book is about making an unconditional commitment to motivational leadership, and how to think like a motivational leader no matter what challenges you and your team are facing.

Throughout this book we will be discussing how to motivate teams as well as individuals. Ultimately, one-on-one motivation has the highest potential, but team motivation also produces significant results.

Why are so many managers not good motivators? The main reason is that most managers don't care that much about motivation. While they might rarely admit it, their priorities are proven by their actions. Many managers are more focused on personal success, achieving tasks or solving problems than on motivating others. They might want the people they are leading to be successful, but they are not sincerely interested in making the commitment it takes to provide motivational leadership. For those managers who are willing to make this commitment, the rewards are enormous in results and in satisfaction.

Whether most managers are sincerely interested in motivation or not, it is one of the most vital elements in leadership, and one of the characteristics which most clearly distinguish great leaders from the rest. Our next chapter will explain what motivational leadership is all about.

Chapter 2

MOTIVATIONAL LEADERSHIP

Developing the ability to motivate others is a huge step toward becoming the kind of leader people want to follow.

Begin by asking yourself this question: Do you find the idea of managing people to be innately positive (as in helping them to be more successful or leading them to a better place) or innately negative (as in personnel problems)? To be an effective motivator, you must develop the first mindset. Leadership is not about convenience or avoidance. It is about taking your followers to a higher level than they could achieve without your leadership. The desire to lead comes from the desire to motivate, and the desire to motivate comes from the heart. You can't fake it or force it. To be a great motivator, you must want to be a great motivator. You must have a true passion for providing positive influence to the world around you. Don't worry about your own success. Commit yourself to the success of your followers, and let your own success be the result.

Once you have resolved this first question, here's the next one: What kind of leader do you want to be? Many people who pursue leadership never earnestly pursue the answer to this question. As a result, their existence as leaders becomes a day-to-day struggle for survival, based more on stimulus and response than on values and vision. Their primary goal is to stay out of trouble by avoiding embarrassment, mistakes or blame.

You must decide *for yourself* what kind of leader you want to be, and what kind of leadership you want to provide. The decisions you make will create the foundation of your integrity as a leader. If you do not take the initiative to make these decisions, someone else will make them for you. You must never let this to happen! It will keep you from fulfilling your unique potential as a leader.

In order to decide the large question of what kind of leader you want to be, begin by asking yourself several smaller questions:

- As a leader, what kind of reputation do you want to have?
- What do you want to provide for your followers that they do not already have?
- What do you want them to provide for you that you do not already have?
- What kind of relationship do you want to have with those you lead? How do you want them to define their relationship with you? Resolve any discrepancies between these two answers.
- What kind of relationships do you want your followers to have with each other?
- What kind of standards do you want to set?
- What kind of atmosphere do you want to create?

This book is designed to help you answer each of these questions. Let's start here with the last one:

What kind of atmosphere do you want to create as a leader?

Answering this question first will make it easier to answer the others.

The most motivational leaders create an atmosphere for their team that includes twenty-two characteristics. We will provide an overview of those characteristics here, and then explain how to bring them to life throughout the rest of this book. Here is the list:

Sincerity

A sincere leader can create a sincere team culture. The title of this book, *Motivation from the Heart,* implies that sincerity will be a dominant theme. If you are perceived as a leader who is sincere, authentic, genuine – who places sincerity among your top priorities in everything you do – it is not hard to instill sincerity in the hearts of those who follow you. Most people want to be treated with sincerity, even those who may not seem sincere themselves. Most people would choose to be sincere if they were not afraid. It is usually fear, not cynicism or dishonesty, that causes people to be insincere. We will discuss how to overcome fear in Chapter Eight. Sincerity is one of the strongest assets of a motivational leader, and of a motivated team culture.

Mutual Trust

Sincerity provides the foundation for an atmosphere of mutual trust. As with sincerity and all of the other characteristics of a motivational environment outlined here, an atmosphere of mutual trust begins with you. It is not only showing your followers that they can trust you, it is also showing that you trust them. They do not have to earn your trust. They already have it. All they have to do is not lose it.

Integrity

An atmosphere of trust requires an atmosphere of integrity. A team with a strong, high-minded value system is more motivated because the values themselves are motivational. Integrity means more than just "telling the truth" or "doing the right thing." It means telling the truth with compassion when it's hard, and doing the right thing when it's risky. Integrity is doing what you say you will do when you say you will do it, even if no one is looking. It means finishing what you start. It means being who you say you are.

Open Communication

Along with integrity, a team culture which encourages honest, open communication nourishes an environment of mutual trust. Your followers need to know where you stand, and you need to know where they stand. While respecting your authority, and acknowledging that the final word is yours, your followers should be encouraged to ask questions or express opposing opinions without fear of backlash, as long as those opinions are not motivated merely by self-interest.

Mutual Understanding

One of the most important elements of any healthy relationship is mutual understanding. Understanding strengthens people's sense of purpose, which in turn increases their motivation.

Creating an atmosphere of mutual understanding begins by giving complete answers and explanations, especially for decisions and strategies. Followers are allowed to question in order to improve their understanding, belief, or sense of purpose. Questions that are not relevant to other team members should be discussed one-on-one with you as opposed to disrupting or prolonging a meeting.

Creating an atmosphere of mutual understanding means you should be interested that your followers understand and believe in what they are being asked to achieve. It also means you should want to understand each of your followers. It takes more time, but builds stronger commitment.

Purpose

Motivation comes from a belief in one's self and purpose. Mutual understanding helps foster a sense of purpose. A sense of purpose produces commitment. A sense of shared purpose among a team produces team commitment, which means loyalty to the purpose and to other members of the team.

The greater a person's sense of purpose, the higher their level of energy and motivation. A leader can make or break a follower's sense of purpose about their mission.

Mutual Encouragement and Reassurance

You are a primary source of encouragement and reassurance to your team. These two important motivational tools often wind up slipping through the cracks in a frenzied world that fixates on results. You need to provide these tools to your followers, who should in turn provide them to each other. People you lead need to know how much you value this concept.

You may be managing a team in which internal competition is an important motivator. Team members may be competing against each other in situations that produce winners and losers within your team. Even in that situation, you will create a more motivating environment when you can maintain an atmosphere of mutual encouragement and reassurance, not only between you and your team, but among the team members themselves.

Self-confidence is one of the most important elements in motivation. You want every member of your team performing at a high level of self-confidence. Their self-confidence will come partly from the encouragement and reassurance you give them.

There are times when you will need encouragement and reassurance from your team as well. You want them to be willing to give it to you because you gave it to them. Your followers will reciprocate what you have given to them.

Mutual Respect

Respect is one of the most important motivators of all. As with mutual trust, creating an environment of mutual respect begins with sincerity. If you have incorporated the first seven elements we have discussed into your team culture, creating mutual respect should not be hard. An environment of respect happens easily and naturally when your team has experienced the benefits of a culture of sincerity, trust, integrity, open communication, mutual understanding, a shared sense of purpose, and mutual encouragement and reassurance.

As with trust, don't make your followers feel as though your respect is something they have to earn. Give it to them unconditionally at first, and most of your followers will not want to lose it.

Mutual Responsibility

An environment of mutual respect leads easily and naturally to an environment of mutual responsibility. Followers know they are responsible to their leaders. It's when they know that their leaders also feel responsible to them that their motivation grows. Showing that you feel responsible to them – and responsible for contributing to their success – makes them feel valued, respected and trusted. While they are ultimately responsible for their own success and happiness, you share in the responsibility for creating the environment and providing the tools that will enable them to succeed.

A sincere sense of mutual responsibility includes a willingness to sacrifice on both sides, and a mutual appreciation when those sacrifices have been made.

Mutual Accountability

Mutual accountability goes hand-in-hand with mutual responsibility. Mutual accountability involves setting the right expectations for each other, and then meeting those expectations. This means making sure your followers understand exactly what your expectations of them are, and how you expect them to fulfill those expectations. It also means agreeing on what expectations they have of you. It requires honest, open communication about whether you are meeting each other's expectations.

Follow Through

Some research lists the failure to follow through as the number one employee complaint about their managers. While a manager's excuse that "I was just too swamped" might seem acceptable to him, poor follow through jeopardizes his reputation for integrity, and undermines many of the other characteristics of a motivational environment we have discussed so far. A commitment to follow through on items that support your team – to finish what you start and do what you say you will do – builds your reputation for integrity and sincerity. This enhances not only your team's respect and trust for you, but also their belief that they are valued, respected and taken seriously.

Vision

Visions are inspiring and energizing. Unfortunately, many managers believe they have neither the time nor the authority to be visionary. Some simply don't give themselves permission to envision. They prefer to define themselves as firefighters and problem solvers. But vision is an important element in motivation, and it is very hard for a "firefighter" to lead or motivate.

Being part of a vision in which we believe is motivating. As a leader you are dealing with vision at five levels:

1. The vision of the organization as a whole.
2. Your vision for yourself.
3. Your vision for your team.
4. Conveying the organization and team visions to your followers.
5. Helping your followers develop a vision for themselves of what they can achieve and how they will do it.

Belief

We have already said that motivation is largely about believing in one's self and in one's purpose. While a large portion of everyone's belief comes from within, leaders can still play a significant role in the belief of their followers. This is called *influence*.

Convey to your followers the principles, values and objectives in which you and your organization believe, and why. Try to identify and nurture the consistencies between these beliefs and those of each of your followers. People are always more motivated when their beliefs align with the purpose they are pursuing and the leaders they are serving.

Then show that you believe in each of your followers, and make sure they understand why.

Passion

Passion is the vehicle through which people fulfill their dreams. It is how they tap resources within themselves beyond what they imagined. Passion is how people exceed the expectations of others, and sometimes even their own expectations of themselves.

To inspire the passion of your followers, you must first let them see your passion for the mission, for your principles, and for leading them. A leader's passion is contagious. It energizes the atmosphere and strengthens the belief and purpose of those who follow. Unfortunately, the lack of passion is contagious as well. When followers see no passion in their leader, their own is diluted.

Energy

Motivational leaders are always sensitive to the energy level of their team as a whole, and of each of its individuals. One way to raise the energy level of your team environment is by radiating your own energy and enthusiasm. But even more important is moderating the balance of energy sources versus energy depleters for your team. If you are focused on creating an environment in which there are more energy sources than depleters, you will have a more energized and motivated team.

As a leader, you have the opportunity to be one of your team's primary energy sources. This means you also have to be careful about managing your own balance of energy sources and depleters. We will show you how to do this, for yourself and for your team, in Chapter Four.

Joy

People are more productive when they enjoy their work and their environment. There are many ways that managers accidentally remove joy from their team's day-to-day experience. You need to be aware of the profound impact enjoyment of work has on the passion, energy, purpose, belief and productivity of your team. The first step in creating an atmosphere for enjoyment is to be aware of its importance. However important and serious the task may be, make it fun and your team will be more energized. They will achieve success faster and sustain it longer.

Relaxed Focus

Relaxed focus is the highest state of performance. A relaxed mind focuses more effectively and performs more efficiently than a mind which is consumed in stress. When you create stress for your team, you reduce its performance.

Of course, a certain amount of stress is inevitable in life. The seriousness of our need to perform can itself be stressful. Our ability to moderate and manage stress significantly improves our performance. Your goal is to help your followers transform their stress into a positive force, so that relaxed focus can be induced, even when they are under severe pressure to perform well, and even when they have to do it in the face of adversity.

Initiative

A motivated environment encourages initiative. Once again, you as the leader set the tone so that your team can follow your example. Encouraging initiative can be a challenge for managers who define themselves more as problem solvers than as leaders. They don't encourage initiative because they want to be heroes. They want to be rescuers, so they perpetuate passive or helpless behavior on the part of their followers.

For some of your followers initiative may not come easily. But as their motivation grows, they will learn that initiative is not as hard or as unpleasant as they thought it would be. The willingness to take initiative is in itself motivating.

Self-sufficiency

Encouraging initiative in those you lead increases their self-sufficiency. Self-sufficiency does not mean being a maverick or "marching to the beat of a different drummer." It does not mean wanting to be left alone. Those are ego issues.

Self-sufficiency means that your followers feel capable and empowered to achieve their own success and master their own challenges. You are there to lead and support, but they are there to achieve and master. When people feel empowered, they feel more self-sufficient and more motivated.

Hope

Hope is another huge energy source, and a major source of motivation. Leaders must convey hope to their followers – a sincere belief that the team's mission is valuable and will succeed. You must have this kind of hope in your own heart in order to convey it to your followers.

To be credible, a leader must be realistic. Hope does not mean blind optimism, but realistic optimism. It does not mean having your head in the clouds. It means having and conveying the assurance that if your team follows your lead their efforts will not be in vain.

But what if you fail in spite of your hope? Failure does not destroy hope, especially when a leader can convey a vision which extends beyond the immediate situation. We are not simply talking about hoping that nothing goes wrong. It is the hope that whatever goes wrong can be made right, and that the end result will be worth the effort.

Consistency

Adaptability and flexibility are important characteristics for a successful person or a successful environment. At the same time, consistency provides stability. A motivational leader balances these two truths so that both function as positive forces.

A leader's decisions need to make sense in the context of previous decisions. The feeling that nothing is consistent can be demotivating. There needs to be a certain amount of predictability for people to maintain their sense of direction, purpose and belief.

Motivation

The final and ultimate answer to the question, "What kind of atmosphere do you want to create?" is an atmosphere of motivation – the only possible result in an environment that includes the first twenty-one characteristics we have discussed.

Once a puzzle is put together, it is no longer a puzzle. It is a completed picture. That's the way it is with these twenty-two characteristics of a motivational environment. Once the first twenty-one pieces are in place, the final piece fits naturally and the completed puzzle becomes a work of art. The element of mystery is gone. You are a leader that people want to follow.

* * *

In their book, *100 Ways to Motivate Others*, Steve Chandler and Scott Richardson quote Lance Secretan as saying: *"Leadership is not so much about technique and methods as it is about opening the heart. Leadership is about inspiration – of oneself and of others...Leadership is not a formula or a program, it is a human activity that comes from the heart and considers the hearts of others"* (Chandler and Richardson 2005, p. 123).

The twenty-two characteristics we have outlined here may seem overwhelming at first – perhaps even unachievable in today's real world. However, there are two reasons why every one of these goals can be achieved by any manager with a genuine heart for motivational leadership.

First, the pieces really do fit together perfectly and naturally. To get the ball rolling, all you need is a mindset committed to motivation. Before long you will find that your team's motivation will begin to take on a momentum of its own.

Second, most of your followers already want these qualities in their culture. Few will resist. Most will embrace them, leaving those who oppose them to become increasingly faint voices in a wilderness of their own making. For the majority, however, you need only to commit to these priorities and demonstrate them yourself. The rest of this book will show you how.

Creating the atmosphere we have outlined here will help you develop answers to the other questions we asked at the beginning of this chapter.

One of the wonderful things about leadership is that you get back from it what you put into it. The level at which you respect, trust and commit to your followers will, for the most part, be reciprocated. If motivating your followers is a top priority, they will want to follow you. If you enrich their lives they will enrich yours. Envision yourself not just as a leader who solves problems and achieves success, but also who motivates your followers – and helps them to motivate themselves.

Part Two

CREATING AN ENVIRONMENT FOR MOTIVATION

CHAPTER

BELIEF

People sacrifice their lives for very few things. Rarely do they sacrifice their lives for money, or a promotion, or a nicer home, or their job, or their favorite sports team. Some people will give their lives for a loved one, and some will give their lives for a belief. Love and belief are powerful motivators. This chapter is about belief – how it motivates people, and how you can use its power to motivate the people you lead.

People will follow a strong leader in whom they believe to places they would not otherwise go. When we talk about belief in a leader, we mean not only confidence in her ability and character, but also confidence in her vision, and in the direction she is taking to pursue that vision. Followers must believe that they are better off with the leader, and they must have confidence that following her will take them to a better place.

People perform at their highest level when they believe in themselves and in their purpose. Belief in self and purpose is motivation in its highest form. It is what motivates people to keep improving.

When we talk about self-belief, we do not mean selfishness, arrogance or godlessness. We are talking about a person's innate belief in who they are and what they can achieve; confidence in their ability to accomplish the task at hand; belief that they are capable of excellence.

When we talk about belief in purpose, we are talking about their sense of mission for the task at hand – how important they believe it is to do the task well.

The greater their belief in themselves, the more powerful and energized their self-confidence will be. The greater their sense of purpose, the more powerful and energized their sense of commitment will be.

The rest of this chapter will explain how to use the power of belief to motivate your team to a higher level of commitment and performance. First we will see how you can inspire them to a higher belief in themselves and their purpose. Then we will consider how to provide a sense of vision and hope that will energize their belief even further.

Belief in Self

The people you lead will have a wide range of self-images. Some people have an innately strong self-image: believing in themselves comes naturally. Perhaps their self-belief comes partly from their awareness that others believe in them. Others will need your help in order to improve their self-image. You will have to teach them how to believe in themselves. You will need to help them with their self-definitions.

Some leaders believe this is more than they signed on for. And yet once you embrace this mission, you will discover that it is one of the most exhilarating and fulfilling aspects of leadership. For reasons beyond your control, you may not succeed every time. Ultimately everyone is responsible for their own self-image. But you can still take your team to a higher level of awareness of who they are, who they can be, and what they can achieve. This could be one of the most important gifts anyone will ever give them.

Raising Self-Esteem

The first step in helping someone with a weak self-image is to show that you believe in them, *and explain why*. People need to hear that they are appreciated by others, and they need to hear the reasons they are appreciated. When this information comes from someone they respect and to whom they are accountable, it is even more valuable. It lifts your followers' spirits and raises their self-esteem when you tell them they're doing a good job. But the impact is even more profound when you can be more specific with a comment like this:

- "I really appreciate the way you…"
- "One thing that really makes you special is…"
- "I've really benefited from knowing you because…"
- "One thing I've learned from you is…"
- "One reason I'm so glad you're on my team is…"
- "One reason I think you're so good at this is…"
- "One way I think you really make a difference is…"
- "One way you've had a positive impact on this team is…"

Our self-image also gets a boost when we learn good things that other people have said about us. Tell your employees compliments you have heard about them.

- "One thing you're known for is…"
- "One thing people say about you is…"

- "One compliment I heard about you that I thought was so cool was…And it really is true."

Generic, vague compliments offer little long-term value for improving a person's self-image. The compliments that make a difference are sincere, truthful, individual and specific. They demonstrate your personal appreciation for who the person is and what they have accomplished.

Sometimes a compliment may focus more on who they *can* be and what they *can* accomplish – compliments about their potential as opposed to their achievements. As long as you give specific reasons why you believe the compliment is valid, it can have profound value.

For example, suppose a new salesperson has gotten discouraged because he hasn't gotten his first sale as quickly as he had hoped. He says to you, "Maybe I made a mistake by thinking I could do this." You could respond by saying, "You just haven't caught your rhythm yet, but you definitely have what it takes. I can see that people trust you and like you, and you set high standards for yourself. I have just as much confidence in you today as I had the day I hired you. You just need to get comfortable with the idea that you're doing something new, and it's going to take a little longer to master it."

For people with low self-esteem, remember that the purpose of your compliments should include:
- Increasing their belief in themselves.
- Motivating them to stretch themselves – to step out of their comfort zone – and commit themselves to pursuing a higher level of excellence.

Improving Self-Definitions

Most people perform at a level that is consistent with their expectations of themselves. Their level of success is determined largely by their own opinion of who they are and what they can achieve. Their performance matches their self-definition. Unfortunately, many people's performance is limited by a self-definition that is below their actual potential, which is why "they always get what they always got." The way your followers define themselves is a major factor in the level of success they achieve.

Our comfort zone is closely aligned with our self-definition. If we insist on staying within our current comfort zone, our self-definition becomes more and more self-limiting. Settling into a self-limiting comfort zone eventually lowers our motivation. Many people deprive themselves of the success they could achieve, and the joy and fulfillment of reaching their potential, because of self-limiting self-definitions. They also miss out on the joy that comes from dreaming, believing and growing.

One of the highest forms of influence you can provide for those you lead is to help them create positive self-definitions. It is well-documented that we tend to become what the people we most admire believe we already are (or can be). This is sometimes known as the Pygmalion Effect. It means our self-definitions are profoundly influenced by the opinions of those we respect. When we see a positive reflection of ourselves in the eyes of people we admire, it strengthens our self-image, raises our self-esteem, and significantly increases our level of motivation. This is where you come in.

Managers can have an enormous impact on the self-image of their employees. One of your purposes as a manager is to help your employees improve their self-definitions where needed. Most people are limited by who they believe they are and what they believe is possible.

Some of your employees will define themselves as second-rate. For whatever reason, that self-definition has become their comfort zone. You need to help them break out of this prison.

Why are some people able to motivate themselves more easily than others? Partly because they have stronger, more positive self-definitions. By helping people to elevate their self-definitions, you can raise their level of motivation and success. The cycle of motivation and success then gains its own momentum. It is one of the most exhilarating cycles in life, and you can play a decisive role in making it happen for many over the course of your management career.

When you show people who harbor negative self-definitions that you believe in them, you are revealing to them that they can accomplish more than they realized. You see not only who they are, but who they can be, and you tell them in ways that strengthen their belief in themselves.

It's From the Heart

Great leaders believe that greatness lies in the heart of every person they lead, however deep that greatness may seem buried. People admire and follow leaders who see their potential – who see the best in them – and who tell them about it. However, we are not talking about encouraging over-inflated egos or a false sense of security. Over time, you teach humility as well as self-confidence. On the one hand, you show your belief in what they can accomplish, and at the same time you also mentor them past the temptation to get a swelled head and then self-destruct.

Everything you tell them has to be the truth. Without sincerity the Pygmalion Effect offers nothing positive. Saying that you believe in an employee rings hollow if you do not also show interest in them. Let them know that you are sincerely interested in who they are and what they think. Ask questions, and then follow up their answers with more questions. Dig deeper. Get them to dig deeper into their own thoughts and values. Show that you appreciate and respect what they say.

If you disagree with them, tell them respectfully. Your purpose is to have deeper, more truthful, more meaningful conversations with your employees, to the extent that time permits.

But can you find the time to do this? You will always find the time to do what you believe is important. Time management is simply a matter of priorities. If you believe that motivation is important, you will find the time to do whatever it takes to motivate your employees to fulfill their potential.

Just as the Pygmalion Effect has wonderful positive potential, it can work the opposite way as well. When a manager believes an employee will fail, it greatly increases the likelihood they will. As much as you may try to be objective and impartial, the way you truly feel about each employee will affect your behavior toward them, and your attitude will find its way into their self-image. This does not mean you bear more responsibility for their success than they do. It means your influence makes a difference.

Even when you don't like an employee or respect their efforts, try to see them as someone with potential for greatness. Show that you believe this potential is really there. Explain why. Show that you truly want to see them fulfill their potential. Explain the steps you believe it will take to get there. Explain what will happen if those steps are not taken. Give them honest feedback about the path they are on and where they could end up. Make sure they understand there is not only an issue of fulfilling their potential, there is also an issue of responsibility and accountability. When necessary, explain the consequences of failing. But show that you still believe in them and see their potential, and give them a vision of their future success. Your goal is still to improve their results by improving their self-definitions.

Regardless of their performance, your mission as a motivational leader is to help them believe in themselves enough to be motivated to take the steps to improve – to pursue excellence and fulfill your vision of who they can be. Help them envision the reputation they could have if they could believe in themselves the way you believe in them.

Belief in Purpose

The level of fulfillment we achieve in our lives – and the level of value we ultimately attribute to our lives – is determined largely by our sense of purpose. The most rewarding periods in our lives are frequently the times when we feel our highest sense of purpose. The periods that seem the emptiest – the times when we feel least valuable – are often when we feel our weakest sense of purpose.

A sense of purpose can be the greatest source of motivation in our lives. It is a vital life force. It brings fulfillment to our lives. A sense of purpose can make or break our motivation – both in individual tasks and in life itself. In their book, *The Power of Full Engagement*, Jim Loehr and Tony Schwartz say, *"Purpose is a unique source of energy and power...it fuels focus, direction, passion and perseverance"* (Loehr and Schwartz 2003, p. 133).

Motivational leaders remain constantly aware of the essential role of purpose in motivation. A lack of purpose drains people's energy. They feel disoriented, unappreciated, less valuable. As a leader you can never lose sight of the connection between a person's sense of purpose and their sense of vitality. A sense of purpose gives them the desire to excel and the will to persevere.

You need to take your role in your followers' sense of purpose very seriously. Help them discover and treasure their sense of purpose. You may even be the one who gives them their sense of purpose. Your encouragement of their purpose is an important source of motivation for them. Encouraging their purpose means to appreciate it, nurture it, support it, and help them live it. You need to help them treasure the fact that they contribute something to the world that no one else does.

Let's go back to the salesman who was discouraged by his slow start. Suppose he elaborates on his discouragement by telling you this: "I was a marketing major in college. I never really planned to go into sales. I tried for four months to get a marketing job, but nothing panned out, so I thought I'd give sales a try. Maybe I'm just not cut out for this." Now you realize that being in sales may represent his failure to achieve his goals.

First, try to find out if he envisions any joy in selling. If he does still envision this joy, but simply hasn't experienced it, and if you still believe he has the potential to succeed, you can encourage him by instilling a greater sense of positive purpose in his new, unexpected career. You could say, "Many people get into sales the way you did, and then wind up liking it better than their original game plan, even if they get off to a slow start. They love developing wonderful relationships with their customers, they are fulfilled by improving people's lives, and they wind up with a better quality of life because of the money they earn once they get rolling. Plus you get to the satisfaction of being the life blood of a company. Don't think of it as an accident that you and this career found each other."

Here's another example of how a manager can encourage a sense of purpose. Suppose the president of your company has volunteered your sales team to spearhead a charity fundraiser. Some of your salespeople complain because it is an intrusion upon either their selling time or their personal time. Convey this message to give them a more positive sense of purpose: "This will be great PR for the company, which is always good for sales. It's a really good work that benefits people, so it might bring you a lot of personal satisfaction. Here's another thing to consider for the bigger picture. One of a salesperson's greatest assets is the ability to step out of your comfort zone and adapt to new things. Think of this as an opportunity to stretch that muscle." If the company could express its appreciation by offering to take the team out to dinner if they meet their goal, that's even better.

Managers who have a hard time motivating their employees are often not conveying a strong enough interest in their employees' sense of purpose. Perhaps they are too concerned with their own success, or perhaps with their own survival. Leaders with charisma don't have this problem.

What is charisma? When we think of the attributes of motivational leaders, we sometimes mistakenly associate charisma with flamboyance. A more important source of charisma is a leader's ability to focus on a purpose higher than herself, and to inspire her followers to do the same. She might say something like this: "We're going to accomplish things that no on else in our market is accomplishing, and here's how we'll do it…Then we'll feel a sense of satisfaction and confidence that no one else in our market has ever felt. It will take the joy of what we do to a whole new level." This is charisma in leadership. It makes her the kind of leader that people want to follow.

People are more motivated to excel when they believe the task they are pursuing truly makes a difference, and that their performance will make a difference as well. Sometimes they realize this by themselves, but sometimes they need to learn it from you. You may be the one who shows them that what they are doing really does have value.

If they are doing good work, let them know it matters. Sometimes just reassuring them that they are making progress is enough to energize them. At the same time, if they are not doing good work, your disappointment needs to be expressed as well. They need to understand the difference in consequences between success and failure. Accountability also plays an important role in a person's sense of purpose.

Combining Efficiency and Understanding

Employees need to understand what they are being asked to accomplish, and what they will need to know and do in order to be successful. At the same time, we have become a society that worships efficiency. Too often we sacrifice understanding at the altar of efficiency, which makes our efficiency very inefficient in the long run. The irony of efficiency is that it takes time to develop. Efficiency only works once proper groundwork has been laid, and that groundwork includes understanding.

Managers often don't take the time to give complete explanations. In fact, they often don't take the time to seek understanding for themselves. Frequently they just pass decisions down the ladder which were handed down to them. The problem comes when they don't pass on the explanation for the decision – the reasoning behind it that creates buy-in. Sometimes managers don't know the reasoning. This knowledge could strengthen the employees' belief in their purpose, which would increase their effectiveness.

Complete explanations create better understanding – the kind of understanding that gives people a stronger sense of purpose by making them feel like a more valuable part of the mission. Short answers may seem more efficient in the short run, but they are less motivating, and reduce the efficiency of the team in the long run.

Motivational managers encourage the curiosity of employees instead of being intimidated by it. Explaining why things are the way they are inspires a higher level of performance and trust.

Your employees need to understand the reasoning and purpose behind decisions and strategies in order to support them. If employees disagree with the purpose or its reasoning, this needs to be resolved. It's not a question of whether employees need to know; it's a question of their motivation and effectiveness. If embracing a purpose increases your team's energy, performance and effectiveness, then it's worth it, even if it requires a little more time and patience. Ignoring the problem will not achieve the goal of higher performance over the long run.

Taking this extra effort also provides you a fringe benefit. When employees see that you go the extra mile to provide understanding and seek buy-in, they will be more inclined to give you the benefit of the doubt when they're feeling skeptical. You have earned their trust and respect, and now they will buy in because you ask them to.

The Stakes Are High

Our sense of purpose plays a role in virtually every conscious act we commit. The stronger our sense of purpose, the more energy and determination we will commit to performing at our highest level. This is why it is so important for your followers to believe that the purpose toward which you are leading them is valuable, that their individual contribution is valuable, and that the quality of their participation will play a significant role in the outcome. When they believe in a specific purpose, it contributes to their larger feeling of overall purpose for their lives, which can have a magnificent snowballing effect for their entire sense of motivation. If their work has value, their lives have value.

We all live for purpose. With purpose we thrive, without it we despair. If your followers believe in their purpose, they have more energy and channel it more productively. If they don't believe in their purpose – or if they don't understand it – morale plummets along with performance.

Morale and performance will also suffer if your followers believe that their purpose conflicts with their core values. If your team believes they are doing something unethical to increase shareholder revenue at the expense of their customers' unfulfilled expectations, their sense of purpose will be compromised. The same is true if they believe they are pursuing a fruitless activity just to cover up a mistake of someone who has previously undermined them. But if they have a misconception, it needs to be corrected.

Is your followers' purpose consistent with their value system? If it is not, this needs to be resolved for the mission to stay on track. Otherwise it is at risk of sabotage, whether deliberate or subconscious. If you have any question about whether this is a problem on your team, ask them. It is an answer you need to know, and it is usually an easy answer to uncover.

A person's belief in their purpose is a high stakes matter. As a leader, you should think of belief in purpose as nothing less than what life is all about.

Consistency of Purposes

Needless to say, people often have more than one purpose at a time, in their work as well as in their lives as a whole. Of course, this is fine. However, as a leader you need to be mindful of two areas of caution. First, be careful that the purposes you are pursuing or assigning do not conflict with each other. Second, be sure that your followers are not jumping too quickly or sporadically from one purpose to the next. And this applies to you as well as to them. Either of these problems can cause anxiety and frustration, which sap the energy that a sense of purpose is supposed to produce.

If your team offers a variety of services, make sure everyone agrees on how these services should be prioritized. Coach them to keep their priorities intact.

When you give employees special assignments as opportunities for possible career growth, make sure they are not distracted away from their core responsibilities. You want them to stretch and grow, but not break, so don't overload them with fringe responsibilities that undermine their basic ones.

Help them distinguish between what is urgent and what is important. A deadline for a report is urgent, and must be met in order to maintain a reputation for reliability. At the same time, committing to a larger plan for fulfilling other responsibilities is important. While reaching a monthly goal is urgent, a commitment to continuous improvement remains important.

Make sure their priorities are consistent with yours. As a leader, you can help them maintain their clarity when other forces are conspiring to create clutter. You may need to provide them with clarity in their priorities when they feel pulled in a variety of directions. This is especially important during times of change or turbulence.

As the leader you set the tone. You will find yourself confronted with these same kinds of decisions regarding your own priorities. You may have to choose between activities that will enhance your own career and those which will increase the success of your team. If you have an opportunity to join a committee that will give you higher visibility and exposure to new challenges, you may want to take advantage of it. However, if the time commitment of this new activity deprives your team of leadership, and their motivation and performance decline, have you really advanced your career? Always protect your core leadership responsibilities – your commitment to the success of your team – and let your own success take care of itself.

Make sure that fulfilling multiple purposes does not undermine your ability to follow through with your own leadership commitments. Even when you are pursuing multiple purposes, you still have to finish what you start and do what you say you'll do in order to maintain the trust of your team.

Success vs. Mastery

One of the characteristics managers hope for in those who work for them is the earnest desire to pursue success.

Motivation From the Heart

But even more extraordinary is the employee who pursues mastery. The desire to achieve mastery in any field or endeavor – to achieve excellence for its own sake and let the success take care of itself – is a much rarer virtue than the desire to achieve success. The pursuit of mastery is a virtue to be encouraged, nourished and mentored.

Many people only seek to be acceptable on the easiest path possible. Some are willing to pursue success as long as the path is not too difficult. Then there are those rare few who choose a more difficult path which requires sacrifice in order to become the best. Keep an eye open for these extraordinary employees. Help them to expand their comfort zone in order to expand the reach of their high standards, and also to provide an inspiring influence for others.

Instill the notion that achieving mastery not only produces the highest level of success but also brings the highest level of satisfaction. The pursuit of mastery turns a profession into a better experience. Those who pursue excellence for its own sake enjoy their work more. We enjoy our work more as we keep getting better at it, and then we keep getting better at it as we enjoy it more. Even when this idea seems obvious, leaders need to express it in order for it to be embraced. Otherwise we can find ourselves so focused on results that we forget the sheer joy of doing something well.

A strong sense of purpose produces success as well as fulfillment. But an even stronger sense of purpose is what produces mastery.

Providing Vision

Vision occurs mentally as well as physically – with our mind as well as our eyes. We are motivated partly by our imagination – by our ability to see with our mental eyes beyond what we can see with our physical eyes. Leaders stimulate the imagination of their followers.

Chandler and Richardson say, *"...one of the most vital aspects of motivating others is the ability to see what's possible instead of just seeing what's happening now"* (Chandler and Richardson 2005, p. 70).

One of the best ways to instill belief in your followers is to inspire them with vision. People want to follow visionary leaders.

Visions are not philosophies. They are vivid images – like photographs of what can be – photographs of the future taken with the camera of your imagination.

How do we develop the ability to envision? First we need to think of it more as an act of will than as a special ability. Everyone has the ability to envision. We all envision *when* we are motivated to envision, and we imagine *what* we are motivated to imagine. Great leaders give their followers a reason to envision and imagine – a motivation to see with their mind what they cannot see with their eyes.

Envisioning is one of the highest forms of creativity. Yet it does not require the mind of an artist or a musician. Athletes from baseball players to golfers to pole vaulters often create a vision of their endeavor before they execute. Many salespeople envision a sale before they make a presentation. The principle of envisioning increases success in any pursuit.

It is hard to convey a vision effectively or credibly unless you can explain how it will be brought to life. An essential part of creating a vision is to create a plan for bringing it to life. This plan must start out general enough and simple enough that you can follow it all the way through in your mind (or on paper). Then you can set about filling in the details of the plan as completely as possible with the knowledge you have. If you need more knowledge to fill in these details, then the next stage in creating the plan would be to acquire this knowledge.

If you as the manager of a sports team have a vision of leading your team to a championship, you might begin by envisioning the championship celebration, with your players taking turns hoisting the trophy. Next envision the team spirit that will put them into a championship frame of mind from the first day of the season. Imagine each individual performance contributing to the total team performance, and play out a complete game in your mind. What will need to change in order for your vision to become real? What new skills and attitudes will each player need to develop in order to fulfill your vision? What can you do to inspire them to make these improvements, and what strategies can you implement to make those improvements happen?

Creating and conveying a vision is one of the ways to show your followers how your leadership will take them to a better place. First you must define your vision to yourself, then decide what kind of leadership you will need to provide. Turn back to the questions we listed at the beginning of Chapter Two for what kind of leader you want to be, and add to those questions several more:

- Envision your team a year from now (or six months or even three months, if those shorter time frames would be more meaningful). How do you envision the team as being different than they are today?
- What kind of team culture do you want to have? (We discussed this with our twenty-two characteristics of a motivational environment in Chapter Two.)
- Now consider individually each person on your team. How do you envision them in the same time period as you chose for the first question above? What differences do you envision from the way they are now? (Your team members will partcipate in answering this question, as we will see below.)

Envisioning can apply to a big picture of the overall direction you want your team to pursue. It can also apply to an individual situation or challenge, where you envision the positive results that can be achieved, and then create a plan for pursuing those results.

Begin with your own vision. Convey it to your followers, along with the specific steps through which it will be fulfilled. Have them share in its creation, and in the steps they will take to get there, to whatever extent is appropriate. They will, after all, play a major role in fulfilling your vision.

Then encourage them to create a vision for themselves, if they don't already have one. As they develop their vision, discuss it with them supportively, conveying interest and encouragement, if you feel that encouragement is appropriate. Talk about how they will get there, and what role you will play to help them get there. You want a shared set of beliefs with them about your vision and theirs.

Sharing a vision with you, whether it is yours or theirs, increases your followers' level of motivation, as long as you agree what part everyone will play in fulfilling the vision.

Your vision as a leader reaches its highest form when it translates into shared goals with a shared plan of action that produces shared motivation.

Providing Hope

Hopelessness is the highest form of despair. All the other forms of despair – loneliness, grief, frustration, futility, depression, fear – can be tempered as long as beneath that despair lies a reservoir of hope. We can persevere through the bitterest adversity when we have hope. In the face of the toughest challenges, hope enables us to surprise ourselves with resources of energy, will, courage, determination and motivation.

Hope often becomes a self-fulfilling prophecy. When we believe good things will happen we feel more energy, and we convey more energy to those around us.

Hope is self-perpetuating. It produces deeper self-trust, a higher level of motivation, and a greater desire to persevere. It gives us more purpose, and it makes life seem easier.

Positive thoughts are a vital part of motivation. You envision positive results in order to achieve them. You motivate others by helping them to envision the positive potential in their challenges. Optimism is a critical element in your success and in the success of those you lead. You and your team will enjoy the journey more if you experience it in a state of hopeful optimism.

As a motivational leader creating an environment of belief for your team, always make sure you are maintaining a demeanor of hope for your followers to see, no matter how difficult the circumstances may be. Followers have more hope when their leader projects a demeanor of optimism and confidence – an assurance that the mission is important and that the team will succeed. Optimism and pessimism are both contagious, and the one you choose will be an important factor in how you are defined as a leader.

Never appear to be whipped. When the present seems overwhelming, rely on the energy of your vision for the future (with its possibilities – its eventual positive results) to provide you with the motivation to motivate your team.

As a leader, you are a vital source of hope for those who follow. Hope begins with you. Have hope yourself, and instill hope in others. Never forget the energy and motivation that hope provides. Hope gives people a reason to believe, improve and excel. For many, it provides the paradigm shift for developing a success mentality.

Motivation From the Heart

Chapter 4

ENERGY

Leaders Are an Energy Source

As a leader, your ability to provide your followers with belief in themselves and in their purpose, with vision, and with hope will establish the foundation for a motivational environment. Whatever internal motivation each of your team members already has, these four gifts from you will nurture and inspire it. They also contribute a vital energy source to your team.

Energy is an essential building block for motivation. An environment of motivation must be an environment of energy. To motivate is to energize. A leader is a team's most important energy source. To fulfill this wonderful purpose, the leader must embrace the responsibility for creating an energized environment.

One of the characteristics of champions is the ability to develop, manage and direct their energy. Mental, emotional and physical energy all play a critical role in success. Energy produces success; success in turn produces energy. It is a wonderful cycle to get caught up in.

As a leader, you are not only an energy source yourself, you are helping your followers to find and develop their own energy sources. This is one more way to become a leader that people want to follow.

If you have never seriously pondered the concept of energy, and how important it is, take the time now. The time you spend learning to understand energy will be a profitable investment. If you can identify and maximize your own energy sources, you will become a more powerful energy source for your followers.

People who radiate a positive attitude and who seek out the good in others provide a wonderful energy source to those around them. You feel more energized after interacting with them. Their very presence makes you feel better about yourself and your situation. As a result, you want to reciprocate these uplifting feelings back to them. In fact, you want to be this kind of energy source to every person you encounter. Whenever an interaction includes positive mutual energy, everyone wins. Tap into the reciprocal nature of energy. Seek out people who energize you, and become the person who energizes others. One of the best ways to increase your own energy is by being an energy source to others.

This principle applies to any kind of relationship. For our purposes here it especially applies to your relationships with your team. Provide them with energy through your own confidence and enthusiasm, your sincere interest in them, and your desire to help them persevere. You will not only energize them, you will empower them. You will give them the enthusiasm, confidence and sense of purpose to continue striving to improve each day.

Beware of people who deplete your energy – those who seek out the worst in everything and everyone. They view adversity as unfair. Discontent seems to be their mood of choice. You can feel the energy being sucked out of you when you are with them. You may be forced to interact with such people, and you can still care about them. But beware to distance yourself emotionally from influences that can deplete your energy. There are times when their negativity can have a seductive appeal. Do not let negative people downgrade your view of yourself, or your purpose, or the abundance of opportunity for joy and success that surrounds you. And beware of those times when you might have the same effect on someone else.

Now let's look at some other ways to energize your team environment. We will consider several forces that increase energy, and we will see how you can make those forces flourish. These positive forces include joy, passion and confidence. Then we will look at negative forces (such as worry, fear and fatigue) that threaten the energy of an environment, and we'll explain how to conquer these forces.

Joy As an Energy Source

Instilling joy is another way to become a leader that people want to follow. If your team feels joy, they will achieve higher performance because they are performing at a higher level of energy.

People who gain the most joy in life realize, at some level of their consciousness, that finding joy is an individual responsibility for everyone. They relate this idea to their lives as a whole, and they relate it to specific situations. Choosing joy is one of the most important decisions we can make in our self-management. It is one of the primary ways to manage our thoughts productively. Leaders must not only embrace this truth, they must convey it through their management style.

The choice to experience joy is one of the greatest blessings in life. It is sad that so many people do not think of it as a choice, but merely as something that happens to them if they're lucky. To get the most out of life, we need to appreciate the extent to which joy is a choice that we really do control. This is one of the key concepts of thought control, and of self-management.

The choice of joy over worry will have an enormous effect on your energy level. The same applies to your followers. Your joy can be an important factor in stimulating theirs.

Joy is a vital energy source. Worry and anxiety deplete your energy, which in turn can create a negative impact on those around you.

Make sure your thoughts are the positive and productive kind that energize you. Don't waste your mental energy on negative thoughts, or on worries about things you cannot control. When you identify a negative or unproductive thought, expose it as the enemy you must conquer. Once you are able to achieve this, you can actually use negative thoughts to trigger positive ones.

Choosing joy takes commitment. Finding the joy in every situation takes perseverance and discipline. We need to be constantly aware of the quality of our thoughts, choosing positive thoughts over negative ones. In layman's terms, focus on the good stuff, not the bad stuff. It is the simplest and most obvious concept on earth, yet it keeps slipping away from us. Those who hold on to it enjoy richer, happier lives. They feel more energized, because positive thinking is a profound energy source. They also provide a more energizing influence on the world around them.

When we look back on ways we have benefited from previous adversities, we can learn ways to welcome future ones, and find possibilities for future joy in our present adversities.

When we say that joy is a commitment, we are talking about the act of will in controlling our thoughts. In our past and present lives, most of us have had a lot to be joyful about, and a lot to be miserable about. Upon which category do we choose to dwell?

We do not have to deny the existence of the negative experiences in our lives in order to focus on the positive ones. In fact, we should focus on the negative ones to the extent that it helps us resolve them, cope with them, or learn from them. However, we can also choose to retrieve our positive thoughts, and allow those positive thoughts to set the tone for our overall state of mind. We can also choose to dwell on the hope of a positive benefit from even the most negative experiences. We can focus on positive thoughts about ourselves and our purpose. What we are talking about here is sometimes known as "self-talk." The quality of our self-talk is a huge factor in the quality of our joy.

Achieving joy includes eliminating thoughts that are not joyful. Identify negative self-talk as an enemy, and unleash the powerful force of your will in order to conquer that enemy.

We may have five good things going on in our lives and one bad thing, yet we may choose to focus on the bad one. If we are focusing on it for the purpose of resolving it, that is fine. But if we are simply dwelling on it with anger and frustration, and no positive purpose or direction, then we are not making the best choice in terms of thought management.

Criticism is a similar situation. We may get five compliments and one criticism and we choose to dwell on the criticism. Is it because we believe that the negative comments about us are truer than the positive ones? Is it fear or insecurity? Whatever provokes this negative focus, we must recognize that it is a distorted, unbalanced perspective of the overall picture. We must also recognize that it is de-energizing. With criticism, we need to gratefully recognize its value for helping us to improve, apply it as necessary, and then let it go. Criticism should serve the purpose of improving our self-definition, not eroding it.

Joy can be about thankfulness. If we focus on those things in our lives for which we should be thankful, we will experience more joy and, as a result, more energy.

Joy can also come from pondering ideas greater than ourselves. We gain more energy when we are focused beyond ourselves than when we are focused on ourselves. When we become absorbed in maintaining and protecting our own well-being, it consumes energy we could be directing into efforts that bring us more joy and greater success.

When leaders appreciate the value of joy as an energy source, and develop the mental discipline to maintain an attitude of joy for themselves, they will provide more energy to their team. In our next chapter we will explain how to create an environment of joy.

Worry

Joy can be undermined by worry. Begin with an awareness that most of your worries are unnecessary. We use up a lot of energy on anxieties that do not improve the outcome.

But what about those times when you really do need to worry? How do you make sure you are "worrying productively?" Even as you are feeling anxious, you need to step outside of the anxiety long enough to evaluate it. Is it moving you toward a positive solution, or is it merely sucking up your energy?

If you can willfully keep your anxiety on a productive, resolution-oriented track, you will be able to bring it to an end once it has served its useful purpose. Let your anxiety run the course it needs to in order for you to decide what course of action to take, and then let it go. Don't rehash the same worry again and again. Worry saps your energy, but resolving it gives you energy.

One source of worry is overanalysis. The expression "paralysis by analysis" refers to the depletion of energy that overanalysis can cause. Analysis can be a very productive activity, but it becomes overanalysis when it is no longer advancing your understanding, or when it is rooted in a self-limiting fear that prevents you from achieving your purpose. The most successful people keep moving forward. Their analysis is rooted in a desire for understanding, not in fear.

Overanalysis could occur as you prepare to introduce a new product into the market. As part of your preparation, you want to identify your target market, research their preferences, decide how you want to reach them, and know your costs. While all of these tasks are necessary, beware of overkill. When fear or lack of confidence produce the desire to keep reevaluating and tweaking indefinitely, you could wind up forfeiting the advantages of getting to the market more quickly.

If you believe you have the tendency to procrastinate through overanalysis, ask yourself these questions at the beginning of the process: "How will I know when I'm ready? Will I ever be completely ready? Is anyone ever really 100% ready to do anything? When will I be ready enough?" If you can envision the state of being "ready enough," it will make you more comfortable taking action without feeling "completely ready."

Salespeople frequently wrestle with this issue. They can always acquire more knowledge, skill and training. But the time comes when they just need to jump in and trust their ability – to perform the task adequately, and to be able to correct whatever they do wrong.

Worry is also an area where self-absorption can rear its head again. As Loehr and Schwartz said in *The Power of Full Engagement:*

"Self-absorption...drains energy and impedes performance. The more pre-occupied we are with our own fears and concerns, the less energy we have available to take positive action" (Loehr and Schwartz 2003, p. 117).

Just as you want to help your followers realize that they will have more energy and success if they can embrace joy and seek out the positive in every situation, you also want to help them realize that their energy will be depleted when they focus on their difficulties.

Passion

When people are passionate about what they pursue, they are virtually unstoppable. They keep going until they accomplish their mission, because they believe the mission is worth it, and that failure is not an option. Passion is a formidable force. It is a vital source of energy for achieving the highest level of success in any endeavor. A leader's dream is a team that has passion for its mission.

Passion comes from belief at the deepest possible level. It cannot be faked. Passion means you believe in something – a principle or a mission or a vision or another person – enough to persevere and sacrifice for your belief. Motivating your followers to this level of passion by conveying a contagious passion of your own is one of the most inspiring forms of influence a leader can provide. It is the kind of influence that enables your followers to surpass their expectations of themselves – to achieve levels of excellence and success beyond what they imagined. It helps them to redefine themselves at a higher and more confident level, which is a profound and priceless gift.

How do you inspire this kind of passion in the people who follow you? Of course, if you have passion for your work and for the mission of your team, that's a great start. If you do have it, why do you have it? The better you can articulate it to yourself, the more effectively you can convey it to your team. Make sure they understand and appreciate the purpose and value of the mission on which you are leading them.

On the other hand, if you don't have this passion, do you know why that is? Did you used to have it? Occasionally passion really does run its course and burn out. But more often the passion that seems to be lost is just covered with clutter. Other distractions, temporary discouragement, negative thought patterns, or fatigue may have covered over your passion temporarily, like autumn leaves on a sidewalk.

But like those leaves, the mental clutter hiding your passion can be swept away.

Recall what inspired your passion, and give yourself permission to relive that inspiration in your mind. Allow yourself to let go of the clutter and enjoy the passion that is rightfully yours. Allow yourself to fulfill the purpose which originally inspired you.

Your goals in creating an environment of passion are to:
1. Have the passion – that vital sense of purpose – yourself (for a great leader this is absolutely essential).
2. Display that passion to others.
3. Instill that passion within them.

Another way to inspire passion in the people you lead is to encourage creative thinking. Passion and creative thinking are closely linked. Passion inspires creative thinking, and creative thinking inspires passion. Individual and team efforts alike are energized when creative thinking is encouraged, appreciated and, when possible, implemented.

A huge part of instilling passion is simply being aware of its importance. Most of the time when leaders fail to instill passion it is for no other reason than that they're just not thinking about it. It is literally an oversight, but it's a pretty big oversight for a leader.

The stronger your sense of purpose, the stronger will be your passion. The same applies to your followers. If you don't feel a strong sense of purpose, you must resolve that in order to be an effective leader. What is it that inhibits your sense of purpose? What can you do about it? What needs to change? Do you need to adapt? Whatever it is – whatever it takes – the effectiveness of your leadership is at stake. Passion is critical to your ability to create a motivational environment.

Passion provides the energy to excel – to do whatever it takes to achieve your mission. It also provides satisfaction and fulfillment from the pursuit of your mission – even during times of adversity or setbacks. With passion you believe that your mission is what you were born to do. You believe it has value. You believe it makes a difference. And you believe you're good at it. Then you are able to pass on this gift of energy, purpose, satisfaction and fulfillment to those who follow you. Now you are a truly motivating leader.

Confidence vs. Fear

Confidence is a great energy source, and fear is an energy depleter. When we talk about fear depleting energy we are talking about the debilitating effects of emotional fear. We're not talking about instinctive fear that generates energy for survival. That is a very different issue. If a tiger chases us down the road it gives us motivation and energy to run fast. But day-to-day emotional fear inhibits and weakens us. Confidence that we will succeed takes us to higher levels of performance than fear that we will fail because we are not good enough.

Let's start with you. Create a clear vision of the successful person you want to be. Success is largely a self-fulfilling prophecy. If you can envision your success and believe in that vision, the rest is perseverance.

Along the way, take time to savor every success you have, no matter how great or small.

Assume that your successes will repeat themselves and that your failures will not, because you will learn from your failures and turn them into future successes. It sounds too simple, but this is exactly what champions do. They assume that their failures are gifts which will lead them to future successes. Champions fail, just like everyone else, but they interpret failures differently. Champions learn from failure without dwelling on it.

We talked earlier about self-definitions. Confidence grows out of positive self-definitions while fear grows out of negative ones. An example of a positive self-definition in sales would be: "I'm a good salesperson because people like me and trust me, and I'm passionate about what I'm selling." A negative self-definition could be: "I don't want customers to think of me as a salesperson because salespeople have a bad image. I just want them to think of me as a friend."

Self-definitions can be even more situation-specific. A golfer who stands over a four-foot putt with a positive self-definition might say, "I love four-foot putts. My stroke is always confident, and that's why I sink them more often than other people." A more negative self-definition might say, "I'm lousy with these putts. I'm great from tee to green, but then I blow it here, and my good shots were for nothing."

Two people could be equally capable of handling a computer issue. However, one could handle the issue more easily than the other if she has a more positive self-definition. The more negative self-definition might sound like this: "I just don't have the right kind of brain for computers." Fear of the computer causes mental clutter that makes the issue harder to master. A more relaxed mind will grasp the issue more easily. The following self-definition can create a more relaxed mental state: "I love new challenges. They make me stronger. Once I master this computer issue, I'll be more confident than ever."

In each of these three situations, the more positive self-definition gains better results through better energy. Negative self-definitions bring the negative energy of fear into play, and results suffer.

The ability to overcome fear is a vital source of energy, just as the fear itself is an energy depleter. As with worry, identify fear and self-doubt as enemies to conquer on the road to success. Conquering these enemies begins with an act of choice and is completed with an act of will.

As a leader you have two goals. First, develop an attitude of confidence for yourself, and second, help your team develop their own confidence. Chapter Eight describes how to do that. Your mission as a leader is to create an environment which inspires confidence instead of fear. This is one of the most misunderstood concepts in management. When we talk about an environment of confidence, we're not talking about a coddling, "I'm-okay-you're-okay" culture. On the contrary, we are talking about an environment of rigorous standards and consistent accountability.

Fatigue

The most obvious enemy of energy is fatigue. Unfortunately some managers, and even their organizations, create an environment of fatigue. There are two ways to avoid this.

First, don't create situations that undermine your employees' ability to manage their energy. An environment of fatigue results when managers run their teams into the ground in an attempt to maximize productivity, or spread them too thin in an effort to maximize efficiency. Maximum productivity and efficiency are achieved when you create the correct balance of exertion and recovery.

Second, teach your employees how to manage their energy. This begins by making sure you are managing your own energy. Teaching your team to manage their energy and avoid fatigue requires leadership by example. So let's talk about your own energy first.

Fatigue can be physical, mental or emotional. How do you overcome these three kinds of fatigue?

Of course, the solution to physical fatigue is rest. The real goal is to try to prevent physical fatigue proactively by getting the right amount of rest on a consistent basis, complemented by nutrition, exercise and relaxation.

You also need to be realistic about pacing yourself. At what point are you pushing yourself past your limits into a counterproductive state? When you feel yourself losing your edge because you have pushed yourself too far, stop and regroup before you begin to lose your perspective. Pushing yourself to your limits only produces growth when it is followed by a period of restoration.

Stress and Recovery

In *The Power of Full Engagement,* Loehr and Schwartz say, "*Our capacity to be fully engaged depends on our ability to periodically disengage*" (Loehr and Scwartz 2003, p. 38). Then they explain the importance of balancing what they call "stress" with what they call "recovery." For our purposes here we can define stress as something which causes us to push ourselves to a point of discomfort – to stretch ourselves beyond our comfortable capacity – and recovery as a period of restoration or recuperation which follows a period of stress. These words from Loehr and Schwartz provide insight for how hard to push yourself or your employees when the goal is optimum performance:

"*The key to expanding capacity is both to push beyond one's ordinary limits and to regularly seek recovery, which is when growth actually occurs*" (Loehr and Schwartz 2003, p. 46)…"*Any form of stress that prompts discomfort has the potential to expand our capacity – physically, mentally, emotionally or spiritually – so long as it is followed by adequate recovery*" (p. 13)…"*Too much energy expenditure without sufficient recovery eventually leads to burnout and breakdown…Too much recovery without sufficient stress leads to atrophy and weakness*" (P. 29).

Stress with recovery leads to growth. Stress without recovery leads to burnout. As a leader, you need to be especially aware of how you provide opportunities for both stress and recovery in a balance that keeps your employees stretching and growing and improving. This means they will be pushing themselves enough to stretch beyond their current comfort zone, and then letting up enough for the growth to take hold and become a permanent part of them. Recovery completes the growth process.

Too much stress for too long a time will destroy their energy by burning them out. On the other hand, too little challenge for too long will destroy their energy through restlessness, frustration and lethargy.

Conquering Mental and Emotional Fatigue

Physical fatigue is usually easy enough to identify. Often the greater challenge is being honest with ourselves about the effect it is having on our performance, and the future effects it could have if we don't make the necessary adjustments.

Mental and emotional fatigue can sometimes be harder to evaluate and resolve than physical fatigue. Causes of mental fatigue can include repetition, loss of intellectual stimulation, frustration, anxiety, failure (or the fear of it), conflict, personal stress outside of work, physical fatigue, and forgetting to focus on joy.

Conquering mental and emotional fatigue begins with identifying it. The most frequent tell-tale symptoms include an increase in irritability, negativity, pessimism, cynicism, impatience, and a reduced ability to focus. Mental fatigue can distort your thoughts. It can sometimes be hard to tell that your thoughts are distorted, so look for the symptoms that we just listed to determine if mental fatigue is setting in. If you see these symptoms in yourself, be open to the possibility that your thoughts could be distorted, and try not to make any critical decisions – especially life-changing ones – until your energy is restored.

How do you restore mental and emotional energy after fatigue has set in? If it is not the result of physical fatigue, consider the following possibilities.

Try to recall any joy you used to feel in your current situation, even through that situation causes fatigue today. Relive in your mind the passion that drove you in the past. Rekindle your previous vision of yourself as an energized and successful champion.

Is the fatigue caused by a lack of balance in your life? When this is the cause, everyone's situation is unique, so focus on what steps you can take immediately to start getting the balance you want. Begin by making sure you know what kind of balance you're trying to achieve. The problem many people have with achieving balance in their lives is that they don't define it. They're not sure what balance is, they just know they don't have it. Decide on your definition of balance before you try to achieve it. Balance must have a specific meaning. It cannot be an abstract concept. Once you have defined it, you can start taking steps to achieve the right balance for you in terms of work, recreation, personal relationships and other personal interests.

If the problem is a loss of intellectual stimulation, decide on ways you can reintroduce this kind of stimulation into your life right away.

Don't neglect the spiritual realm either. However you address spiritualism in your life, remember its importance as a source of energy.

What about your day-to-day life at work? How can you rekindle your energy and passion from one moment to the next when you don't have the luxury of a vacation, or when it will take some time to re-establish the kinds of balance described above? If you can't take a physical vacation, you can at least take mental breaks between interactions and challenges. One of the remarkable things about the mind is its ability to retreat into a relaxed mode at a number of different moments each day. It takes a little mental discipline, and anyone can do it. You can find several opportunities each day to take your mind wherever you want it to go – to a place of joy, a place of peace, a place of rest. Then you can bring it back when you need to. During these mental breaks, think about things that are relaxing, interesting, positive and energizing.

If there is a place where you can retreat physically as well as mentally, that is even better. Changing your physical environment helps you change your mental environment. A park is ideal, but going for a walk or visiting a shopping center, coffee shop or library can also work. Even a place inside your office building can re-energize you if it gives you a feeling of separation from your normal work environment.

Relaxation is not merely restful, it is a rejuvenating energy source. Think about the things that bring you joy. Think about anything positive you expect to experience in the near future. We are talking about an issue over which we all have as much control as we want – the issue of choices and thought management.

In this chapter we are not talking about energy in terms of science, but in terms of motivation. As a leader you can help your followers understand how to apply the principles and techniques we have discussed here. Create an environment that encourages energy, and help your followers to manage their energy in ways that will make them more productive. Embrace the idea that the more energized your team is, the more motivated they will be. The more motivated they are, the more energized they will be.

Energy is a resource to be managed diligently. Managing energy requires that we make correct choices about how we will maximize our energy sources and minimize our energy depleters. Energy is not something that just happens to us. Those who learn how to manufacture and protect their own mental, emotional and physical energy can develop one more competitive advantage over those whose attitude toward energy is more complacent. Make sure that everyone who follows you appreciates their own role in energy management, and make sure you embrace your role as an important energy source.

Motivation From the Heart

CHAPTER 5

CREATING AN ENVIRONMENT OF JOY

In our last chapter, we talked about joy as a source of energy and motivation – for teams as well as individuals. In this chapter we will explain how to create a team culture that lives and breathes joy, and how this team culture increases motivation to achieve maximum performance.

Have Fun

One way to experience joy is by having fun. So let's begin by taking a look at what Anne Bruce and James S. Pepitone say about the connection between fun and motivation in an organization. From their book, *Motivating Employees:*

"Employees who are having fun at work might well be exhibiting the single most important trait of highly effective and successful organizations...There's a direct correlation between fun on the job and employee productivity, creativity, morale,

satisfaction, and, most of all, retention – not to mention greater customer satisfaction and a host of other benefits…In a work environment that encourages fun, employees have:
- *Lots of energy,*
- *Greater self-esteem,*
- *Enthusiasm for their work,*
- *Team spirit,*
- *Sustainable motivation, and*
- *Positive attitudes"* (Bruce and Pepitone 1999, p. 89-90).

Bruce and Pepitone then list "10 Characteristics of Fun:"
1. *Humor alleviates stress and tension.*
2. *Fun improves communication.*
3. *Fun eases conflict.*
4. *Laughter can help us survive.*
5. *Laughing at yourself is the highest form of humor.*
6. *Laughter has natural healing power.*
7. *Humor helps lighten the load.*
8. *Fun unites people.*
9. *Fun breaks up boredom and fatigue.*
10. *Fun creates energy* (Bruce and Pepitone 1999, p. 91).

When a leader has a sense of humor, it can help to shape the team culture in a wholesome way. Here's what Bruce and Pepitone say about humor:

"Humor helps us put things into perspective. When you encourage people to have a sense of humor about their work, it forces them to take a step backward from the situation at hand. When they do that, they can usually see more clearly and in more detail everything surrounding the situation" (Bruce and Pepitone 1999, p. 90).

The emotional benefits of fun are connected to physical benefits. Once more, from Bruce and Pepitone:

"Fun is motivating because of the pleasure it creates. It stimulates the pituitary gland, which produces endorphins and enkephalins. These are natural painkillers that are 100 times more powerful than morphine! So when employees or managers are feeling down, stressed, tired, or just not in the mood to work up to their abilities, a laugh can make a big difference" (Bruce and Pepitone 1999, p. 90).

The environment you create can be serious without being somber. Seriousness of purpose is just as important for success as fun is. You can have a strong sense of purpose and have fun pursuing it. In fact, a strong sense of purpose usually makes work more enjoyable. People enjoy their work more when they have a sense of direction and feel that their work is important than when they feel as though they are adrift. They also enjoy their work more when they are improving, and they keep improving when they are enjoying their work.

When you lead a team meeting, maintain your sense of humor and welcome the humor of others, as long as it does not undermine the direction of the meeting. Including fun and imaginative activities can also make your meetings more productive.

When you are meeting your employees one on one, include some laughs. Show that you enjoy your work, even if you are going through a rough patch, and help your employees to experience the joy of theirs. Some employees don't believe they have permission to feel joy, especially if they are underperforming. While they have to take seriously the standards to which they are being held, make sure they have permission to enjoy their work, as long as they are also focused on the mission at hand and the standards to which they must perform.

Provide recreational opportunities for your team to enjoy each other's company. Consider a quarterly schedule for recreational team bonding. These occasions offer tremendous motivational value by enabling co-workers to socialize and provide mutual support. If you can attach these occasions to group achievements, it adds one more reason for mutual support and congratulation among the members of your team.

If you have a hard time coming up with ideas for these energizing occasions, it's okay to ask your team members for help. You can even ask them to take responsibility for part of it if they are more imaginative and gifted in the fun department than you are. Don't neglect these important opportunities for enjoyment just because you think you're "not the fun type." It's not about you, it's about your team. Stepping out of your comfort zone will be good for you, too.

Of course, creating a joyous atmosphere means much more than just having fun. The rest of this chapter will explore some other dimensions of an environment of joy.

Convey Optimism

People will enjoy any situation more when they believe it's going to work out. Optimism is an important element in an environment of joy. Even in a team meeting where you have to focus on what's wrong, do it in a way that gives hope for the future.

How do you create an enjoyable environment when times are hard? Even in a negative situation you can create a positive track. We have talked about the importance of vision in motivational leadership. Tough times require vision. Provide your team with a vision for a positive outcome, and an action plan for achieving that outcome. Your followers need to envision a happy ending for whatever tribulation they are enduring. They also need to believe that their leader has them on a path to a better future.

To provide this kind of leadership, you must have the attitude that adversity is a gift provided to help us break through to the next level of excellence. It is the vehicle through which we develop new skills, strengths and attitudes that don't develop in normal times or good times. Seeking growth during tough times enables us to prosper during the better times, and to handle the best times with grace and perspective. Your goal is to find the gift in every adversity.

Whenever you have to discuss a difficult situation – with an individual or with your team – go into it prepared. The theme of your presentation, and of your leadership during challenging times is, "Here's our situation. Here's what we need to do, and if we do it, we'll be fine."

There may be times when you feel that such a guarantee is inappropriate, and could erode your credibility if your plan doesn't work. You may even feel as though your plan is nothing more than grasping at straws. In these situations you can still reassure them that even though they may have to try several things, you won't give up until you have prevailed. You'll get through it, and when you do, everyone who perseveres will be better because of it. Imagine that your goal is for your followers to say of you, "He's unstoppable," or, "She will do whatever it takes, and as long as we hang in there with her, we'll come out fine in the end."

Make them know that their efforts will be worth it. Show your own optimism, and your enthusiasm for embracing the challenge. Show your confidence that even if you're not sure of the answer, through perseverance you and your team will find it. Let them know that you are shoulder to shoulder with them all the way.

Help them to think long-term by reminding them, "These are the times that you will look back on with tremendous satisfaction as you tell the story of your success."

Look for opportunities to express how much you appreciate their efforts and perseverance.

Encourage their imagination. The opportunity for imagination is another gift that lies within adversity. We often get our best ideas when our backs are to the wall.

When a team brainstorms a strategy for attacking a challenge, energy and optimism can emerge in a variety of ways. People become more hopeful that they will prevail over the adversity. They feel more empowered because they are thinking outside the box. They feel more excited as they feed off each other's creative energy. They feel less helpless as they envision solutions. They are moving away from an attitude of, "This situation is making us miserable," toward an attitude of, "There's a solution to everything, we just need to find it." They no longer feel doomed. Victory lies ahead.

This kind of team imagination also stimulates individual imagination. People appreciate that new ideas lead to new victories, and they can be the one to come up with those ideas.

We imagine when we become motivated to imagine.

Be aware of the kind of energy you convey. You are one of the team's primary energy sources during times of adversity or change. Loehr and Schwartz emphasize the influence of a leader's positive energy and emotions when they say:

"The ability to communicate consistently positive energy lies at the heart of effective management" (Loehr and Schwartz 2003, p. 75)..."*The ability to summon positive emotions during periods of intense stress lies at the heart of effective leadership"* (p. 92).

We have been focusing on times of adversity, but conveying optimism, positive thinking and positive energy is just as important in good times. Taking optimism for granted when times are good can leave your employees feeling unappreciated and unfulfilled. Good times can have challenges of their own, such as poor communication. People often have to work hard, be creative, take initiative and incur inconvenience in good times as well as bad. Let them know that they are valuable in the good times, too.

Maintain a Healthy Perspective

Some of your employees may need your help finding the good in a tough situation. Is the glass really half full or half empty? Finding the gift in every adversity is one way to help your followers maintain a healthy perspective for whatever situation they face.

Is a competitive situation an opportunity to win or to lose?

Is adversity an inconvenience or an opportunity to set yourself apart from the rest of the pack?

Will change make things worse or better? Often change is a self-fulfilling prophecy. It makes things worse for people who think it will be worse, and better for those who think it will be better. Which way of thinking will you choose?

You may be better at maintaining a healthy perspective than some of the people who work for you. Perhaps that's how you became their boss in the first place. Don't get exasperated with them too quickly. Give them an opportunity to embrace a new perspective, to learn new ways to maximize their new opportunities.

Suppose you have to dismiss an employee for providing poor service to customers, and reassign his customers to a different employee. She may express displeasure at first. She may even criticize you for giving her an unfair situation. She needs to learn a new perspective. Perhaps no one has ever taught her that embracing this kind of challenge can be immensely rewarding. Since the customers were served poorly by the previous employee, they will frequently be all the more appreciative when a new person turns the situation around. Her reputation within the company will be enhanced more than if she had never been given the opportunity to handle a difficult situation that was caused by someone else. If she chooses to resist and continue to complain about unfairness, she is admitting she will only accept an easy path, and is placing herself in a category which is not too different from the person she's replacing.

Perspective is an area in which your influence can make a decisive difference. Perhaps a healthier perspective can be developed through greater understanding – through an explanation of why things are the way they are – why a decision is what it is. A healthier, wiser perspective often grows from understanding the reasoning behind a decision, direction or strategy. This is especially true during times of change.

Make sure that you and your followers agree on what's important and why. Even though you're the boss, they will be more motivated if their priorities align with yours. When theirs are different, hear them out. Maybe they are making a point that really is important – one which you didn't think of. Or maybe they just need a better explanation from you. Differences in priorities can often be reconciled.

Compatible priorities reduce worry, anxiety and fear. They also reduce complexity and mental clutter. If your followers believe that their actions are fulfilling your priorities, it strengthens their confidence that their efforts will be appreciated. But they need to be comfortable with your priorities. It's okay to ask, "Are you comfortable with the direction we are going?" You're not asking for advice on how to do your job, you are valuing their opinion. Plus, if they're not comfortable with the direction, you have the opportunity to motivate them differently to alleviate their discomfort.

We discussed the importance of humor in creating an environment for joy. Humor is also important for maintaining a healthy perspective. The ability to make light of difficulties or setbacks in an appropriate way, without making light of anyone's individual misfortune, can reduce stress. It reminds everyone that a setback is not the end of the world. We live in an imperfect world, and there truly is an element of humor in that. The good news is that an unhappy story can still have a happy ending if we hang in there and do whatever it takes to make it right.

When faced with a disappointment, we can choose one of two attitudes. We can view the setback as the end of the story. Or we can view the setback as a part of a story that is still evolving. It is important to be aware that most situations are evolving, and that our response to the challenge can influence the outcome. Let the situation play itself out, and continue to pursue the best possible result. Rarely does a situation pass beyond redemption. Most can be salvaged if the people involved want it to be. Maintaining a healthy perspective requires long-term, big picture thinking. Because you are the leader, creating this perspective starts with you.

In addition to long-term thinking, you also need to coach employees about thinking in the moment, and how to strike the balance between these two ways of thinking. An example of balancing these two attitudes occurs when an industry experiences a tough market. Employees need to think long-term in order to see beyond the challenge to the solution, and to life beyond the challenge. At the same time, they cannot fixate on the problem so that it consumes them. You can counsel them when to move their focus away from the tough market and live in the moment, in order to gain the most from each small opportunity until the market improves. Help them to think about the opportunities the moment offers. These opportunities include not only the task itself (such as making a sale), but building a reputation for weathering adversity and providing a positive influence to others. For long-term thinking, you can help them envision the larger payoff once the tough times have passed.

Promote an Atmosphere of Relaxation

Relaxation is the highest state of performance. A relaxed mind performs more efficiently than a tense mind. A relaxed demeanor has a more favorable effect on others than a tense demeanor. In sports, being in the zone is the ultimate state of relaxation. You want your employees to be in the zone as much as possible.

However, achieving excellence also requires a certain amount of intensity. Does this create a problem? Can you have the intensity you need in order to excel when you are in a state of relaxation? Absolutely. Intensity and relaxation are totally compatible. In fact, they enhance each other. We will go into detail about how this works in Chapter Nine – *Teaching Relaxed Focus*. At that point we will also explain how leaders can create relaxed focus in their team culture. Here we are focusing on the idea that relaxation accompanies fun, optimism and a healthy perspective in the list of attitudes your team needs to develop in order to achieve an environment of joy. All four of the ideas we have discussed so far in this chapter fit perfectly with each other. They go hand in hand, and each one makes the other three more effective.

As with fun, optimism and a healthy perspective, your demeanor sets the tone for an atmosphere of relaxation. If you show up for a team meeting looking stressed out, exhausted or whipped, the tension in the room rises and the confidence and energy fall.

Be on the lookout for employees who are stressed out. They may not admit it at first, to you or even to themselves. But if you see signs that stress is taking a toll on them, you can talk with them in a sensitive way, and help them explore different perspectives on their situation that may reduce their stress. Left unresolved, there is a risk that the stress will continue to get worse, but helping the employee address it can pave the way to a quicker recovery.

To be relaxed does not mean you are taking your mission any less seriously. It means that your mission will not be diminished by anxiety or fear. Whatever your team is experiencing has been experienced before. Whatever adversity they are experiencing will pass. Whatever challenge they are facing will be conquered. Whatever anxiety they are feeling can be worked through and managed. Whatever success and joy they are feeling can be preserved and built upon.

Leaders often find one or two followers that they feel comfortable confiding in. This is normal. These followers have earned such trust from the leader that he will confide in them his fears, worries and frustrations. There are times when pursuing this course with a trusted follower will help you to resolve your challenges, while energizing the follower with a sense of his own unique value and contribution. In these situations, however, you need to remain aware of the effect you are having on the follower. Make sure you are not sapping his energy, optimism or enjoyment, or preventing him from experiencing his own relaxed state. Of course, you also need to be cautious about confiding sensitive information that could be used against you if the confidant decides to turn on you.

Relaxation is not a lack of focus, and it is not a lack of energy. It is the state in which focus and energy can be brought to life in its highest form.

Promote Team Spirit

All of the elements of an enjoyable environment come to life more powerfully when there is a strong team spirit among your followers.

Team spirit means that each individual puts the well-being of the team before his own. This is a lofty ideal that can never be perfectly achieved. Regardless of how far your team may now be from this ideal, you can still create an environment where team spirit prevails. But how can you get your followers to buy into this idea?

As a motivational leader who sets the tone, begin by showing your trust that if you take care of them, they will take care of you. You are not waiting for them to take the first step. You are taking it.

Show special appreciation for those members of your team who take care of their fellow team members through an effort or sacrifice of their own. Don't reward behavior that goes against this ideal.

Take advantage of opportunities to take care of your team (one at a time or as a group), and show your appreciation when they do the same. It will not take too long for this idea to catch on with the majority because for them the upside of embracing this idea is much greater than the downside. It benefits individuals as well as the team. One important disclaimer, however: When we say to look for appropriate opportunities to take care of your team, we don't mean giving them whatever they want. We mean helping them when you truly think it's the right thing to do, when they are fulfilling their responsibilities to the best of their ability, and when it will not hurt the rest of the team.

If a salesperson faces huge obstacles which his peers don't face, and no one else wants to trade places with him, raising his commission rate may be the right thing to do. However, if the problem is just that he needs help figuring out a solution, then before giving him a pay raise, explain the challenge to the rest of the team and ask everyone to share what approach they would take in his position. Give appreciative recognition to good ideas. This may turn out to be a process that the team looks forward to, whether to get help with their challenges or to gain a reputation as a person of vision who helps others.

The point is to create an environment in which people *want* to take care of each other because they understand the benefits to everyone. Even the most hardened, self-centered cynic experiences more joy when he is focused on a purpose higher than himself. He just sometimes needs help and encouragement in order to take that step outside of his comfort zone.

Those who are too selfish or afraid or insecure to embrace this concept eventually become the outsiders, and fail to reap the rewards of the camaraderie. You can have private conversations with these employees in which you encourage and counsel them about the benefits of embracing a team spirit and the risks of rejecting it. Take the other initiatives first, so that everyone has a chance to buy in on their own or with the help of their peers.

To whatever extent possible, show your employees in a one-on-one setting that you sincerely care about each of them. Of course, if you are managing a huge number of people, you may only be able to focus on those who report directly to you. However, by doing this you can also convey their responsibility to do the same for those who report to them.

Set team goals and offer team rewards for achieving those goals. You certainly want to reward individual achievements as well, but be sure you balance them with team achievements.

There is no reason why team goals should conflict with your mission of instilling a competitive spirit within each of your employees. Sports teams are a great example of this. Each member of the team wants to achieve the best individual statistics possible, but not at the expense of the team. You see frequent examples in sports where a player is willing to sacrifice an individual opportunity, statistic, record or reward in order to allow a situation in which the team as a whole will benefit. Why is he willing to make this sacrifice? Is it just for the good of team? No, there is a pragmatic element is well. He realizes that in addition to benefiting the team, the sacrifice will also benefit him by gaining him a better reputation, as well as the future support of his team members when the time comes for them to step up to the plate for him.

Another example of team spirit co-existing with competitive spirit is a team culture in which your employees want to share best practices and help each other improve, while still striving individually to maintain their own competitive edge. They work together to raise the bar for the team as a whole, but each still tries to be the best.

When employees come to you to complain about another employee, counsel them on how to resolve the issue with the co-worker themselves. Don't just tell them to do it. Tell them *how* to do it. That may be the real problem. They don't want to confront the employee because they don't know how.

Maintain a standard where you are insisting on an environment of mutual understanding, mutual responsibility and accountability, mutual communication, mutual support and mutual loyalty. Explain to your followers that you consider the pursuit of these ideals to be virtuous, and failure to pursue them to be below the minimum standard for the team.

Let them know that their contribution to this ideal will be valuable. Explain that living up to this concept will be an important part of the reputation they develop, the influence they have, and the legacy they will leave. Revisit the issue of their self-definition. What kind of person do they really want to be? Encourage them with your vision of the person you think they can be. Don't just criticize them; give them a vision of something better, and a way to fulfill that vision.

Establish the Right Balance of Compassion and Accountability

How does an enjoyable environment affect accountability? Do your employees eventually become less accountable when you are trying to keep the atmosphere fun, relaxed and positive? Keep in mind that an environment where everyone fulfills their responsibilities is much more enjoyable than one where they don't. When your team is not held accountable – to you and to each other – the environment deteriorates into one of mistrust and grievances. Those who don't uphold the standards don't succeed, while those who do uphold the standards ask, "What's the point?" Both groups become less motivated.

An environment of joy requires the correct balance of compassion and accountability. You are seeking to create a culture that prizes mutual caring. You care about each member of your team, they care about you, and they care about each other. But this attitude of caring implies that everyone is committed to the standard for the good of everyone else.

On the compassion side of the equation, you want to be sensitive to the well-being of your team. If people are not enjoying their work, you need to know why and you need to want to fix it. You need to work through the issues that threaten an environment of enjoyment until those issues are resolved, either through understanding or through change. You never lose sight of your responsibility for the well-being of your team. Just as you pursue your goals as a team, you also protect your group culture as a team. You welcome open, honest communication as long as it is productive and not motivated by a personal agenda. Then you say, "Here's how we're going to master this challenge together."

If a new policy requires people to make sacrifices, be straightforward in your explanation: "Yes, we will have to make sacrifices, but here's why it's so important…" If the complaint is that the policy is unfair, give a thorough explanation of why it's not. You may have to say, "We all want a policy to be fair for us individually. But fairness can be complicated. Try defining fairness without using any first-person pronouns. Sometimes the closest we can come to being fair is to have a policy that is equally unfair to everyone. We are asking everyone to be equally unselfish, and that's fair."

However, if you cannot offer a persuasive argument, or if you personally believe the policy is unfair, don't just say, "There's nothing I can do. It's company policy." Instead say, "Let me look into this further. I'll come back to you with a more complete answer by _____ (commit to a deadline)." This buys you time to learn more about the reasoning for the policy, or state your concerns, or at least have time to think the situation through more completely.

If the problem involves another department, don't let yourself and your team play the role of victim. If you believe your team should accept a ruling that favors another department, explain why you believe it is the right thing to do, and what your team can do to make the situation better. If you think the ruling or policy is wrong, go to your counterpart in the other department and plead your case. You might at least come to a mutual understanding, make a compromise, or elicit a promise of future support when your team needs help in a different matter. In any event, when you say you will pursue a matter, do it as promptly as possible. Your reputation for credibility is very much at stake in situations like this.

On the accountability side, remember that your team expects you to hold them accountable. They know that's what good leaders do. Of course, they expect you to hold everyone else accountable as well.

If you are uncompassionate, you lose respect. You become a leader that no one wants to follow. But if you don't commit yourself and your team to a standard of mutual accountability, the same thing happens. You lose respect, and people stop following you. Your team is responsible for upholding the standard, and everyone knows it, whether they actually adhere to it or not. At the same time, you are responsible for enforcing the standard, and everyone knows that as well.

If you let accountability slip away, you reward those who ignore the standard at the expense of those who uphold it. People will have more fun in an environment where everyone carries their weight. A higher level of mutual accountability creates a higher level of mutual respect and trust, just as a higher level of compassion does. It is the combination that ties it all together.

Keep Politics and Intrigue to a Minimum

The final step in creating an enjoyable environment is to aggressively attack any forces that undermine this environment. When unwholesome politics or agendas cause intrigue within your team, resolve this intrigue quickly. Left unchecked, it can become one of the most sinister forces undermining motivation. It causes mental clutter, increases anxiety and saps energy. It takes people's focus off of their higher purpose and the well-being of the team.

If the problem is caused by grievances over policies, then the policies need to be discussed until mutual understanding is achieved. Sometimes mutual agreement is impossible, but that's not the real problem. That's a part of everyday life. Solutions lie in the realm of understanding. Resolution is achieved when everyone understands why the policy exists and, if the policy will not change, then deciding whether they will stay or leave. The one option they do not have is to stay and infect the culture with personal grievances.

If the problem is caused by an employee, then the necessary conversation must take place, even if it is uncomfortable. One of the greatest risks to a team's culture is its leader's unwillingness to confront an employee who is threatening the team's motivation or its mission.

We will not go any farther with this idea here, since this chapter is about creating an environment of enjoyment. However, our next chapter will explain how to create an environment of trust. We will discuss the importance of communication, and describe how to handle necessary confrontations in a way that maintains trust and improves motivation.

Motivation From the Heart

Chapter 6

MOTIVATION WITH HIGH STANDARDS

Being part of a team with high standards is a powerful source of motivation. High standards can enrich every aspect of motivation we have discussed so far – belief in self and purpose, energy and enjoyment – and then take your team's motivation to an even higher level.

Most people want to live in a world of high standards – even when they are afraid of the responsibility. As a leader you can help your followers to embrace high standards in a way that helps them resolve these mixed feelings of dignity and fear. You can lead in a way that shows them how high standards are truly their friend and not their enemy.

In this chapter we will begin by explaining how to create a value system with which your followers can identify. Then we will show how this value system inspires a team culture where high standards are the driving force.

Establishing a Value System

Each person's values are an important part of their identity – a vital ingredient in their self-definition. We all define ourselves partly in terms of our values: what we believe; what we stand for; what ideals or purposes are most important to us; what it is about ourselves that we are not willing to compromise or let go of. If we wrote down who we think we are, and then how we would like to be described, the combination of those two statements would express our values.

When people feel clear and secure in their values, they have a greater sense of purpose. They feel more motivated, courageous, confident, energized, directed and empowered. They are more likely to set goals, and they are more likely to achieve those goals.

When we refer to a person's set of values, we often call it a "value system." The term "system" implies an *integrated* set of values – a set of standards, morals, ethics, ideas, and ideals that all work together and support each other. When people's values conflict, it causes anxiety and disorientation. When they are in harmony they create a strong sense of purpose and motivation. Values give us strength, confidence and energy. When we are able to sincerely live out a system of values that are harmonious with one another, we gain fulfillment.

This state of harmonious values is also known as *congruence of values*. We need congruence of values in order for our value system to truly take root and become the day-to-day core of our lives. When we don't have congruence of values, the inconsistencies need to be resolved in order for us to reach our full potential and to achieve the full satisfaction that life offers.

All of these principles for congruence of values apply to teams and organizations in the same way they apply to individuals. When a team's values conflict (or even appear to conflict) with each other, it creates corporate anxiety. Employees will sometimes use harsh terms, like hypocrisy, to define these incongruities. It dramatically reduces a team's sense of purpose and its level of motivation. When a company declares that customer satisfaction is a top priority, and then falls short in its commitments to customers in order to increase profitability, employees as well as customers become cynical. Employees also become cynical when a company says it welcomes their ideas but then does not respond to those ideas.

In addition to congruence within the individual's and the organization's value systems, there is a third kind of congruence that is essential to motivation. This is the congruence between the individual's values and the organization's values. The greater the harmony between the values of an individual and the values of the organization he serves, the stronger will be his sense of purpose and the higher will be his level of motivation.

A leader that people want to follow expresses a value system that motivates the team. The value system you express will be more motivating if it is congruent with the values they already have. If their own value system is vague, then they will be motivated if you can express a value system to which they can aspire.

As a leader, understanding the values of the people you manage helps you to help them integrate the values of the organization with their own individual values. The more you understand their values, the more you can help them appreciate the congruence between their values and the mission of the organization.

If they feel that you are requiring behavior from them that is inconsistent with their values, this incongruity will not only affect their own motivation, it can cause them to have a negative effect on the motivation of others. Suppose a company attracts employees by proclaiming a "God first, family second, job third" value system. Employees with these same priorities are motivated by congruence between the company's values and their own. Later, the company seems to encourage (or at least turn a blind eye to) dishonesty, and also demands continuous overtime, including days off. Of course, longer hours are sometimes necessary to meet an unusual challenge. However, when the company condones dishonesty for profit and takes time away from their employees' commitments to worship and family, the CEO can expect plenty of eye rolling the next time he touts high-minded corporate values.

The better you understand the personal values and motivations of your employees, the better you can help them connect the mission you are assigning them to their own values. If the incongruity between their values and their mission on your team cannot be resolved, then it does neither of you any good for the relationship to continue. If an employee is not comfortable with the values by which you are leading, explain the value system you have embraced for your team in a way that makes it as appealing as possible to the employee. If he chooses to reject it, either by his words or by his behavior, then your team is not the right team for him.

Congruence between the values of the individual and the team is important. So is open-mindedness and sensitivity to the values of your employees. Who knows, they may have something to teach you and the rest of the team. However, the pursuit of congruence must never tempt you to compromise the group value system to appease an individual, especially when the individual does not meet the standards you have set for the team. You are the leader. You set the tone. You express the value system, and then lead by example. Don't lower your standards in order to achieve congruence. Just be mindful of the importance of congruence for the motivation of the team. When you see incongruence, hear people out. Then resolve the issue as quickly and clearly as possible.

For example, suppose you want to have a contest in order to provide short term motivation to achieve a goal. An employee who doesn't like competition may try to convince you that competition lowers morale because "it brings out the worst in people." Instead of sympathizing with their uncompetitive nature, encourage them to embrace the opportunity to expand their comfort zone, and the satisfaction of stretching and growing that competition provides.

It all starts with you. Make sure your own values are congruent with your behavior and with the mission you are leading.

What kind of value system do you want to create? What kind of standards do you want to define that you and your followers will uphold? What will be your team's code of ethics?

As a leader you want to establish:
- Standards that will lead your team to its desired goals.
- Standards that will enhance every team member's belief in themselves and in their purpose.
- Standards that will produce a desire on the part of every team member to improve every day.
- A value system in which they can take pride.

- A set of values to which your best employees already aspire.
- Values that will make them proud to say, "I belong to this team because…" and, "I follow this leader because…"

One of the great things about having higher standards, once people buy into them, is that higher standards lead to higher motivation. Higher motivation in turn leads to higher standards. On the other hand, lower motivation and lower standards also nurture each other. Your role as a leader is to advance the former cycle and eliminate the latter one.

Through your leadership you articulate and uphold the standards you set for the team. You lead by example. Your team will be motivated if they respect your standards and see you living them. But they need to know what you value and what you stand for. This, of course, begins with you knowing what you value and stand for.

How do you articulate the standard?

First, you lead by example. Second, put the standards into words. An explanation of the standards and the reasoning behind them is a good place to start. A written mission statement, or even a slogan, can help the most fundamental standards become part of your team's code.

The next step is to gain agreement from your followers. They need to express their commitment to the standards just as surely as you need to express yours. If they agree, they have to live up to it. If they don't, you need to resolve it. Don't let too much grey area develop between these two alternatives. They either live up to the standards or they don't. The more grey you allow this area to become, the more grey it will become. Both the value system and the motivation of the team will suffer.

Now let's define the kind of value system that produces motivation. Our definition includes the elements of integrity, selflessness, goals, initiative and self-sufficiency.

Integrity

If you ask one hundred people whether they would rather live a life of high integrity, medium integrity or low integrity, at least ninety-five would say high integrity. So why don't they do it? Usually it's because they're afraid. Maybe it's fear of loss: they'll miss out; someone else who takes a path of less integrity will get the jump on them. They could be afraid that a path of integrity really won't lead anywhere. Perhaps they feel it's just too risky, or that they'll alienate people. Often it's a fear of confrontation. Sometimes it's the cynical fear that integrity doesn't truly get rewarded in the real world – only in fairy tales.

The irony in all of this is that integrity is one of the best ways to conquer fear. Standing up for what you believe is very liberating. You feel stronger. You feel more confident. Why? Because you like yourself better. Integrity has the power to conquer fear, and yet we allow our integrity to succumb to fear.

An example of integrity conquering fear would be admitting a mistake. Suppose Bill makes a mistake that could have negative consequences for someone else. However, he knows a way to sweep the mistake under the rug, at least temporarily, so that no one could ever trace it back to him. He's afraid that if he admits the mistake he will lose the confidence of his peers and managers. However, he can build a better reputation by admitting the mistake than by hiding it (even if no one ever finds out that he made the mistake or covered it up). He will be known as a person who can be trusted, and who will make right what he does wrong. Everyone makes mistakes. Our reputations are based not so much on what we do wrong, but on what we do to make it right. Once Bill embraces this concept, he experiences the satisfaction that comes from the triumph of integrity over fear.

    To create a value system of integrity, you have to give people "permission" to have integrity. By that we mean show them with real proof that they will be better off when they exhibit integrity. You don't just encourage integrity, you recognize it when it happens beyond the call of duty, and reward it when you can. This does not mean giving them a cash bonus every time they tell the truth. But convey to them your admiration, respect and appreciation for their act of integrity, especially if courage has been involved. Show them that it means something to you – that it puts them in a special category of character.

    Suppose you offer Ann a bonus for a special accomplishment. However, she knows that she did not really earn the bonus, because credit for the accomplishment belongs to someone else who recently left the company. She tells you this, knowing that her bonus will go up in smoke. Even though you don't give her the bonus, tell Ann how much you admire the fact that she sacrificed a bonus in order to uphold the principle of integrity.

    Be sure you never punish integrity by penalizing it. Ann was not penalized for her integrity. She simply did not get a bonus to which she was not entitled. Bill should not be penalized either, at least not for his integrity, even if he must face consequences for the mistake he made.

    If an employee confesses an error, you may have to administer negative consequences for the error, but find some positive consequence that you can offer for their honesty. Respect is often reward enough. After all, it's a big one. They still have to correct the problem they have caused to whatever extent they can, but let them know that their reputation with you includes integrity, and that integrity is a reputation worth having in the eyes of everyone else as well. Ultimately, their reputation, like yours, is more important than any cash reward, plaque or promotion. As a leader, you know that your reputation can make or break you. They need to realize that the same is true with them. What you prize more than anything else in an employee is a good reputation – a reputation for integrity. Make sure they hear this message loud and clear.

An environment of integrity is one in which:

- People tell the truth. And they are comfortable telling the truth, as long as they are telling it in a constructive, positive, productive and selfless way.
- People are willing to take their self-interest out of the equation in order to determine the right thing to do. Selflessness will be our next topic.
- People do what they say they will do, when they say they will do it.
- Mutual trust is a dominant theme. You trust them, they trust you, and they trust each other.

Let's look at how the attitude of selflessness fits into the value system you want to create.

Selflessness

Selflessness is one of the make-or-break ingredients for strong team values. We are more motivated when we are living for a purpose higher than ourselves. We perform better when we focus on our mission than when we focus on ourselves.

Unfortunately, as with integrity, many people are afraid to give selflessness a try. They put themselves first because they are afraid not to. The good news is that for those who are able to break out of the miserable prison of selfishness, their feelings of fulfillment move to a higher level.

Most people have the virtue of selflessness within them. They just need courage to live it, and you can help them find that courage. Developing the courage to live by one's values is very motivational, especially when combined with living for a purpose higher than one's self.

Mentoring is an example of selflessness when it is volunteered without compensation. Mentors give their time and effort to help someone else, while a more selfish person would say, "I'm not being paid for it," or, "I'm not stupid enough to work for free just to train my replacement (or future competitor)."

You will not be able to cure the disease of selfishness single-handedly, even for the people who work for you, but you can still make a difference. You can show them that you put their well-being before your own. Leading by example, you can help them to embrace the belief that for good people with good reputations, good things will eventually happen.

As a leader, show them how the mission which the team is pursuing has value, and how their individual contributions have value, too. Assure them that the quality of their efforts has value beyond their own well-being. If they uphold the values and standards you have set for the team, they really will make a difference which benefits others as well as themselves. If they see that you have a passion for these values, they will be more motivated as long as they believe in you, and in your commitment to do whatever you can to take care of them. Just as you care for them, you can inspire them to care for each other. Everyone wins with a value system driven by selflessness.

Commitment to Goals

Does commitment to goals belong in this section on values? Absolutely. Goals define your team's purpose, and a commitment to achieving them is a crucial part of your team's value system. Whether it is a sports team or a business team or a military team, goals are one of the reasons the team exists. One of the purposes for cultivating the other values that run throughout this book is to achieve goals.

We discussed the importance of congruence earlier. It applies here, too. Your goals need to be congruent with your values.

Goals motivate us to develop the all-important *"What will it take?" mentality* that is one of the defining characteristics of successful people. Successful people are willing to do things that other people are unwilling to do in order to achieve their goals. This does not mean crossing ethical boundaries. That is where the congruent values of integrity and selflessness come in. A "What will it take?" mentality is simply a "no excuses" mentality. You don't ask, "Will I succeed or fail?" You ask, "What will it take to succeed?"

Your goals not only provide purpose, they unify your team in the pursuit of that purpose. You inspire and lead the attitude of *mutual support* for pursuing your goals until you achieve them.

Some goals are tangible and measurable, making success easy to define. Then there are other goals – often less tangible – toward which you lead your team for the sheer pursuit of excellence, enrichment and fulfillment. These intangible goals are often the ones that really motivate you to improve each day – helping you to achieve your measurable goals, improve your life and enrich your team environment. Our next topic is an example. You could set a goal to help each member of your team learn how to take more initiative and achieve a higher level of self-sufficiency.

Initiative and Self-Sufficiency

We have combined these two elements of a value system as one topic because of the close connection between them. If you can nurture initiative among your followers, over time it will evolve naturally and wholesomely into self-sufficiency.

Self-sufficiency is not the same as selfishness or survivalism. Quite the opposite. It is the initiative to resolve anything that is within their sphere of responsibility. It is an attitude of confidence that will make them more successful. It will also make your job easier and your time more productive.

We all wish for a team filled with people who take initiative by themselves. Some people seem to be born with it, while others seem as though they will never have it. They just don't seem to have the interest, energy or aptitude. Can initiative be taught or inspired, or can it only be demanded? It may be more difficult with some of your followers than others, but initiative can be taught and inspired.

As with the other elements of an environment of high standards, teaching and inspiring initiative begins at the leadership level. Your initiative will show them the way, and inspire them to pursue its benefits. Let's look at three ways to demonstrate to your followers the kind of initiative you expect from them.

The first way is to demonstrate your *willingness to make sacrifices* (to do things that others would be unwilling to do – to exceed the expectations others have of you). If you put extra time into helping people in other departments, even when they have been reluctant to support yours, you are taking the lead to improve communication and cooperation between the teams. Your goal here is to inspire in your team a willingness to go beyond job descriptions and assigned responsibilities. To adopt the attitude of "What will it take?" instead of, "What if I can't?" Show your willingness to go the extra mile to help co-workers at your level as well as those who work for you. Show that you are willing to ask them, "What do you need from me in order to become more successful?"

A second way to demonstrate initiative is to show your *willingness to solve problems*. This does not mean becoming an enabler for people who lack initiative. It means showing them how to solve problems so they can do it for themselves next time. Your goal is for your followers to feel confident to bring you their own suggested solutions when explaining a problem. You might encourage them by asking, "What would you do if you were in my position?"

You are teaching your followers to think for themselves. By showing your own initiative in the area of problem solving, you can now ask them to take more responsibility in the areas of their individual challenges. This is a huge part of creating an environment of motivation with high standards. It is where initiative evolves into self-sufficiency.

The third way to demonstrate initiative is through your *willingness to communicate*. We will discuss communication later in this chapter.

Once you set the tone for initiative by your own example, you can lead your followers to raise the bar for their own initiative. Here are several ways to do this.

Keep the concept of initiative and responsibility reciprocal between you and your followers, as well as with team members who are at your level. Once you ask, "What do you need from me?" you can now ask them to reciprocate: "Now here's what I need from you."

Look for opportunities to recognize the initiative of your people. Verbal recognition, in public and in private, shows that you not only ask for initiative, but genuinely value it when your request is honored. You may even consider an award for "Initiative of the Month." Another way to reward initiative is to give more latitude and autonomy to those who are ready to take greater ownership of their responsibilities.

Teaching initiative includes teaching caution. One of the dangers of initiative comes when people only think a plan half way through. As you encourage your people to take initiative, and even to take risks in some cases, you must also teach them to think a plan through to its conclusion. This includes envisioning the possible range of consequences.

For many people this is a growth process which they must take one step at a time. In the early stages, make sure they collaborate with you on their ideas, so you can evaluate their plans and teach them how the thought process works. Help them to evaluate the balance of risk and reward, and to project results. As they show signs of progress, you can expand their latitude and risk level.

Any time you encourage growth and initiative, there may be an element of risk for you. This is why many managers do not encourage initiative – they are afraid of the personal risk. What if something backfires? Getting past this fear requires a commitment to the big picture. Unfortunately, failure is one of the risks of initiative. On the other hand, rebounding from failures is one of the most valuable kinds of success your employees can achieve. While they must bear the consequences for failures and bad decisions, they should also be spared the pain of ridicule, as long as they took genuine ownership of the situation, and now take responsibility for the failure. As a manager, you can monitor the risk closely enough to show your employees that the value of initiative is still greater than the price of small stumbles along the way.

In this section we explained 4 elements that create a motivational value system for your team:
- Integrity.
- Selflessness.
- Commitment to goals.
- Initiative and self-sufficiency.

Now let's go a step farther in creating an environment that motivates through high standards. Let's talk about how to create an environment of trust.

Creating an Environment of Trust

Sincerity

Motivation increases in an environment of trust. The key to building trust is sincerity.

Chip Bell, in his book, *Managers as Mentors*, cites research from his partner Ron Zemke which concludes that "*Trust, according to Zemke, is a blend of authenticity (genu-

ineness), credibility (reliability), and communication" (Bell 2002, p. 41). Sincerity is the quality that unites these three elements of trust and brings them to life.

"Insincere sincerity" has been tried often, and it just doesn't work. There's no way to fake sincerity. You either have it or you don't.

People are motivated when others (especially their leader) show sincere interest in them. Insincerity in a leader produces cynicism in followers. Cynicism is a serious enemy of motivation.

People are also more motivated when they are taken seriously. When they are not taken seriously, feelings of discouragement can destroy motivation.

If you want your followers to trust you, begin by showing that you trust them. Don't make them earn your trust first. Go ahead and give it unconditionally, and let your trust be theirs to lose rather than to gain. The principle also applies to respect. If you want them to respect you, respect them first. If you want them to be sincere with you, be sincere with them. If you want them to take an interest in you and in what you want, take an interest in them and what they want. If you want them to take you seriously, take them seriously. Why should you be the one to take all this initiative? Because you are the leader. You set the standards, and you set the tone. This is how you become a leader that people want to follow. It is how you create loyalty. Loyalty to a sincere leader is a much deeper and more powerful motivator than obedience to authority.

Let us re-emphasize: sincerity is not just treating people respectfully. It is not just taking people seriously. It is being sincerely interested in them: what it will take to make them successful; what it will take to make them feel fulfilled; how to help them pursue that fulfillment.

Sincerity motivates people by giving them dignity.

Truthfulness

Chandler and Richardson state that, *"Great leaders...tell the truth faster than other managers do"* (Chandler and Richardson 2005, p. 42). That's an interesting way of putting it. It's not just about getting around to telling the truth eventually. It's feeling a sense of urgency about it.

Truthfulness is more than just honesty. Unfortunately, many people choose to define honesty as the absence of lies. As long as you're not lying, you're being honest. Sometimes truthfulness is harder than that. It can mean telling someone something that they don't want to hear, and something you don't want to say. It can create an uncomfortable situation that you would rather avoid. Yet the other person needs to know the truth in order to improve. Remember, you're creating motivation. True motivation includes the desire to improve every day.

Most people really do want to know the truth, whatever it is. In fact, one of the frequent complaints employees have about their managers is that they don't tell the truth when they need to. The problem that many people have with the truth, however, is that they don't want to *hear* it. This is a paradox that needs to be resolved: People want to know the truth but they don't want to hear it.

How do you resolve this paradox? Envision the positive possibilities that can result from the employee knowing the truth. Sometimes the truth hurts at first, but if it's constructive the initial hurt passes soon enough, and hurt is replaced by gratitude to the person who was willing to put himself in the uncomfortable position of telling the truth. Of course, this is not the same as criticizing just for the sake of making oneself feel superior.

Many managers back off from truthfulness because they are uncomfortable with confrontation. They worry that they may lose control. We will address how to handle confrontation shortly. For now, the point we want to make is that you will have a better reputation as a leader if you are truthful, even when it's hard. That really is what your followers expect from you, and they will respect you for doing it, especially when it's hard. After all, they know it's uncomfortable for you as well as for them. If necessary, explain to them that you are fulfilling two responsibilities:

1. To protect the standards of your team.
2. To help them achieve their highest potential – to be the best they can be.

As a leader, once you have respectfully and compassionately confronted an employee with the truth, let them know you are ready to help. Leaders offer followers a wonderful resource for perspective as well as technique.

Sometimes we need to conquer our own fears in order to be truthful, but surrendering to these fears can be very costly. In the long run, we have much less to fear when we are being truthful. A truthful leader will be rewarded with a reputation for integrity, for high standards, and for caring about the well-being of her followers.

Encourage truthfulness from your followers as well – to you and to their other team members. However, their truthfulness needs to be respectful, compassionate and constructive. Truthfulness is unlikely to have a positive influence unless it conveys a positive and necessary purpose. Loehr and Schwartz say, *"Truth without compassion is cruelty – to others and to ourselves"* (Loehr and Schwartz 2003, p. 164).

Tell your followers that you value this virtue of truthfulness – that it is an essential part of the value system you are asking them to uphold.

Responsibility

Another complaint that is frequently voiced by employees is their manager's unwillingness to take responsibility. They feel their manager will grab any credit within his reach, whether he's entitled to it or not, while he keeps responsibility at arm's length. This is a harsh assessment, and an ironic one. You would assume that the one thing leaders would be good at is taking responsibility. Isn't that how they got to be leaders in the first place? But the truth is that some people find the responsibilities of leadership harder and more intimidating than they bargained for. Yet taking responsibility is one of the initiatives followers most want to see. It is also one of the initiatives that are most important for creating an environment of high standards.

Taking responsibility does not require micromanagement, but it does require a clearheaded sense of priorities. First and foremost, remember that you are a role model. If you want your followers to embrace a high standard of responsibility, know that you are the standard by which the ideal is defined.

As a role model, it is more important to take responsibility than credit. Let credit come to you on its own path. To the extent that you do take credit, take blame just as honestly. Even when you have a legitimate excuse for a failure, address the excuse in the spirit of, "What can I do better next time?"

If it is right to blame someone else (and sometimes it is in order to improve the future result), do it in a constructive way: "What I will need for you to do differently next time is…" You don't have to cover yourself with sackcloth and ashes saying, "It's all my fault," when it isn't. Let responsibility land where it belongs. The old "I blame myself for your failure" routine is not always constructive. Sometimes it's nothing more than manipulation.

One of the most important objectives in taking responsibility is to create an environment of *mutual responsibility*. Commit to your followers the responsibilities you will uphold, and give them permission to hold you accountable for those responsibilities. Then define their responsibilities to you, to the organization and to each other, and your intention to hold them accountable to these responsibilities. This will make you the kind of leader that people want to follow, and the kind for whom they want to excel. They will want to protect your well-being as well as for their own.

Chandler and Richardson make the following point about mutual responsibility:

*"A leader is compassionate, and always seeks to understand the feelings of others. But a leader does not try to **manage** those feelings. A leader, instead, manages agreements. A leader creates agreements with team members and enters into those agreements on an adult-to-adult basis…When adults agree to keep their agreements with each other, it leads to a more openly accountable company culture. It leads to higher levels of self-responsibility and self-respect…It frees up communication to be more honest, open and complete"* (Chandler and Richardson 2005, p. 51-52).

It's okay to make mistakes (although it's not okay to make the same mistake over and over). Mistakes can lead to improvement. If you do make a mistake, just say, "I made a mistake. I'll apply what I learned so I can do a better job next time." If there were negative consequences to your mistake, take your medicine. Don't look for a place to hide. "I know I let you down with the mistake I made. I apologize. You deserve better, and I'll give it to you in the future." If there is something that needs to be made right, say that, too. "I need to make this right, and I will. What I'm going to do is…"

You don't want to act overly humble or overly confident. Just play it straight. As Chip Bell says, *"Humility and confidence are equal partners in engendering trust"* (Bell 2002, p. 44).

Let's look a little closer at how to make accountability a positive force for motivating your followers through an environment of high standards.

Creating an Environment of Accountability

Accountability goes hand in hand with responsibility. You and your employees are accountable to each other. You not only have to fulfill your mutual responsibilities and commitments, but also answer for them.

Mutual Accountability

The most motivating environments are those in which responsibility, accountability, respect, trust and support go both ways. They are mutual values which are reciprocated. Our recurring theme appears again: the leader sets the tone. You provide a support system for the team; in return, they become a support system for you.

However, the leader is also in the position of authority. Everyone must uphold the mutual standards, but you are the one who must enforce them. Can mutual accountability go hand in hand with authority? Let's see how it works.

Set the tone by saying to your team, "Here's what I need from you. What do you need from me?" This does not mean you have to give them everything they want. But you do have to give them a thoughtful, informative answer. Sometimes they will express needs or request change simply because they don't understand why things are the way they are.

Once the mutual responsibilities are defined, you close the loop with a commitment. This sounds obvious, but it is actually where the breakdown often occurs, when responsibilities are defined more clearly than commitments. A complete commitment says:

- Here's what I will do.
- Here's how I will do it.
- Here's when I will get it done.
- You have my word, and you can count on it.

This kind of commitment puts integrity on the line – serious business in an environment of high standards.

You may have employees who complain that it's unfair for your team to have higher standards than other teams. Question them on that. "Why do you feel that it's unfair for us to have a higher standard? Do we not have the right to improve? Someone has to lead the way. Why shouldn't it be us? Why shouldn't we be proud to do it? Leading the way to higher standards is a cool thing. It's an honor – a privilege.

Don't you want to be a part of that?" Don't let them use someone else's lower standards as an excuse to lower yours.

Discipline

The subject of accountability winds up including the unpleasant topic of discipline. Think about that for a moment. Why is discipline an unpleasant topic? Think of the all the wonderful benefits discipline offers. These benefits include:
- Self-control leading to greater self-confidence and ultimately to the joy of self-mastery.
- Skills and routines that increase efficiency.
- A higher level of fairness.
- A higher level of mutual respect, trust, support, responsibility and accountability.
- An environment that makes higher standards more real, credible and achievable.

Discipline is not dictatorship or martial law. We're talking about an idea that is innately wholesome – a higher level of reliability, fairness and purpose. So what is it that gives the word "discipline" a bad connotation and makes it a topic we want to avoid? Is it because sometimes enforcing it is unpleasant? Let's fix that now.

Addressing the Need to Improve

When you have to confront an employee whose attitude, behavior or performance is not up to the team's standard, take comfort in the fact that this is what your followers expect you to do. They know you are protecting the well-being of the team. They know that upholding the standard is your responsibility. It may feel uncomfortable when you have to do it, but in the long run it will become much more uncomfortable if you don't. Failing to enforce your standards with those who don't uphold them is not fair to those who do.

What about motivation? Will negative feedback de-motivate the employee who is already discouraged? There's no reason it needs to be that way. When you have to address a negative issue, consider several ideas.

Most importantly, remember that in order for the employee to improve, motivation must be part of the solution. You have to maintain accountability for poor performance, but be careful about de-motivating an employee when you most need to motivate him. When you have to deliver a tough message, or even consequences for not improving, remember that their self-confidence is still vital to their future success.

Let your employee know that you still believe in him, and why. Provide encouragement and reassurance, even if you put him on notice. Of course, you do not want to reassure someone that he will be protected even if he doesn't improve. You can provide reassurance of your belief in his ability to succeed, and your hope that he will.

Give him a vision of who he can be. When telling him how he needs to improve, you can use words that are gentle and hopeful, but still serious in their purpose. For example, "What I wish for you, Joe, is…" Notice we described the person Joe needs to become in order to meet the standard.

Balance support with accountability by saying, "I believe you can do it, Joe, but I need for you to do it."

Get feedback and closure: "Can do you do that, Joe?" ("Will you do that?") ("Are you willing to do that?")

Then tell Joe what will happen if he doesn't improve.

Bring trust into play when you have to. If he makes a

commitment to you and then doesn't honor it, let him know that you take commitments seriously. Tell him, "You made a commitment to me, and you didn't honor it. Where do we go from here?" Or you can simply say, "I need to know that you take your commitments seriously." Or, "I need to know that when you make a commitment I can trust you to honor it."

You can be supportive but also severe – compassionate but firm. Joe's motivation is that you believe in him and can tell him how to succeed. Recognizing the consequences of failure can help your challenged employee find the motivation to succeed.

Handling Confrontation

Fear of confrontation is a dangerous weakness in a manager. While you may never feel comfortable confronting an employee, you should never fear it. When it cannot be avoided, you need to welcome and embrace it as a way to achieve mutual understanding and resolution. Both professionally and personally, people who enjoy confrontation often damage their relationships. On the other hand, when necessary conversations are avoided, relationships suffer as mutual respect and trust erode.

To develop a fearless thought process about confrontation, let's consider vocabulary. The very word "confrontation" has an intimidating sound to it. Suppose we substitute the positive words "conversation to achieve resolution."

Approaching confrontation with a positive attitude is more likely to produce a positive result. Embrace it as the best avenue for achieving resolution. Why assume it will have an unhappy ending? Assume a happy ending instead. If you approach it as potentially positive – achieving results that benefit everyone – it can eventually become a productive and satisfying endeavor.

One problem most of us have with confrontation is that we think more about ourselves than the other person. We want to make sure we come out okay. We tend to think more about winning than resolving the problem. This worry for our own well-being becomes a source of weakness.

One way to become stronger in confrontation is to avoid worrying about yourself. Worry about getting the other person through it instead. Say to yourself, "When this is over, I'll be fine. I need to help the other person get through it so she'll be fine, too." The goal is to preserve her dignity as well as your own.

Suppose you must resolve an employee issue of attitude, performance or behavior. Plan your conversation in advance as completely as possible. Decide how you will begin, anticipate the employee's possible range of responses, then plan your responses to hers. While you cannot predict the entire conversation exactly as it will happen, this should give you a good start to help maintain your control and confidence.

Assume the employee wants to achieve positive resolution just as much as you do. If she does not, she puts her future at risk, and she knows it.

Don't try to rush the conversation. Use time as your friend, not your enemy. Give the employee the time she needs to talk through her feelings. It is very important for confrontations to be complete conversations in order to achieve closure and resolution. View the confrontation as an opportunity to accomplish something positive and valuable, not as something that needs to end as quickly as possible.

With all of the demands on your time, it may seem as though you cannot afford the luxury of long conversations. While your time is at a premium, these conversations are a vital part of leadership. The quality of the relationship, and perhaps even the success of the employee's career, are sometimes determined by conversations such as these. Unnecessary damage can result when they are aborted or abbreviated because of discomfort.

Employees need to know where they stand, and usually they want to know. While they may not want criticism, the alternative is living in a vacuum, or with a false impression of how they perceived. As we said earlier, they want to know the truth even when they don't want to hear it.

Don't try to skate during confrontations. Be direct. You can often achieve your most satisfying outcomes when you are willing to fly straight into the storm. Once the storm blows over, the employee will appreciate your directness, and your own confidence for handling future confrontations will increase.

You do not have to wield authority in a confrontation with an employee – at least not at first. Your authority is implicit. You can afford to sit back and take an open, unthreatening approach, until you realize that approach is futile. Usually it is not. After all, you are the boss, so the employee is the one who has to fix the problem. You don't have to worry about winning. You only have to worry about achieving mutual understanding, and then moving forward to a solution.

Let the employee know that you respect him, and help him feel comfortable saying what is really on his mind. There is nothing weak about saying, "Tell me if you think I'm wrong."

Occasionally a conversation of this type may continue for a couple of hours, but it may be the most valuable task you accomplish that day. You may salvage a career, or inspire a new self-definition or sense of purpose in your employee. Give the conversation the time it needs. Patience is important here. So often you feel a sense of futility after the first hour, and then tremendous satisfaction at the end of the second. It may take an hour for the "issues behind the issues" to surface, and for mutual trust in these awkward circumstances to develop. The conversation may take an entirely new direction that is better than either of you imagined, as a whole new way of resolving the problem suddenly appears.

The worst feelings an employee can experience in this kind of situation are humiliation and ridicule. Be sincere, and show that you are taking him seriously. It is important to give your employee confidence. He is not the enemy, and you are not trying to conquer him. You both want the same things – his success and a good relationship between the two of you.

Having said all of this, there will still be times when you feel the confrontation just isn't working. Perhaps the employee is digging in his heels and being defensive, rather than showing respect or an open-minded desire to improve. You need to stay firm in your resolve. You planned what you wanted to achieve, and you cannot afford for the confrontation to end with an unclear sense of purpose. Here are three possible directions you could take under these circumstances.

First ask, "What would you do if you were in my position?" This forces the employee to step outside of himself and consider the impact of his attitude, performance and behavior on the others with whom he works. Throughout the conversation you have been trying to understand his position. Now it is time for him to understand yours. Hopefully he will realize that for you to allow him to continue on his current course would be negligent and detrimental to the rest of the team.

Secondly say, "I'm only asking you to adhere to the same standard that everyone else does."

Thirdly, if you continue to run into a brick wall, you may finally have to say, "We don't seem to be getting anywhere. You need to decide if this is the right company (team) for you. If it is, then you will need to _____ [tell him what you require, and the timetable on which you will evaluate his progress]. If this is not for you, then the sooner we resolve it, the better it will be for everyone."

Communication

The way you communicate to your followers, through your words and your behavior, will greatly affect their motivation, and their perception of you as a leader.

In order to motivate your team to reach higher standards, you must communicate a commitment to the goal of *mutual understanding.* To convey understanding is, after all, one of the most basic purposes of communication. However, we also put a high premium on efficiency. If we can master efficiency, we will become more productive and more successful.

Efficiency is important, but so is mutual understanding. For too many teams communication has been wounded in the crossfire as we take aim at ever more aggressive targets for efficiency. Effective leaders strike the correct balance between these priorities. They know it takes a little longer to communicate in a way that creates mutual understanding, and they don't cut corners in communication just to save time. When leaders don't take time to create understanding that motivates, they will wind up squandering much more time than they saved, and also get lower results. Complete communication – the kind that creates mutual understanding and motivation – takes more time but is also more efficient.

A manager may say, "I gave them the information they need." But was the information complete and accurate? And did he give them the understanding they need in order to pursue their task with belief in self and purpose? The more clearly your followers understand something, the more powerfully they can be motivated by it.

Communication is a vital part of the support system that your followers expect and need you to provide. The quality of your communication goes a long way toward defining you as a leader, especially a motivational leader.

As a motivational leader, what is it that you want to communicate, and how do want you want to do it?

Information, Decisions and Answers – with Explanations

One of the primary characteristics that distinguish us from all other creatures is our desire for knowledge and understanding. We are uniquely driven to find answers to the questions "What?" "Why?" and "How?" The answers to these questions help to shape the nature of our motivation.

Employees frequently complain that they cannot succeed because they don't have the information they need, or they can't get a decision from their boss, or they can't get an explanation of why the decision is the right thing to do. While these can be an expression of the employee's own lack of initiative, they are often legitimate complaints.

Knowledge inspires motivation, and motivation stirs a desire for more knowledge. Our desire for understanding parallels our desire for knowledge. We not only want to know *what* something is, but *why* it is the way it is. We want to know *what* to do, and also *how* to do it. If a soldier understands why it is so important to stop an enemy, he will fight more vigorously and sacrifice more willingly. If he has been taught how to fight more effectively than the enemy, it's even better.

If you provide your followers with the knowledge and understanding to succeed, they will be more motivated to achieve their objectives. On the other hand, if you deprive them of knowledge and understanding, you undermine one of the distinctive human motivators.

The first step is to give your followers the information, answers and decisions they need *when they need it*. (Providing the right information at the wrong time is a poor solution to a communication problem.)

Then offer explanations that make the information powerful by giving it reason and purpose. So often followers don't buy into an idea, a piece of information, a decision or a strategy because they don't understand it. They grumble and spread dissatisfaction to other team members because they don't realize the reasoning and purpose behind the information.

People need to know how to accomplish a task, but the level of excellence at which they perform the task results more from their sense of purpose than from their knowledge. As a leader, when you provide knowledge, make sure you instill a sense of purpose that inspires performance at the highest level.

In addition to information, decisions, answers and explanations, let's look at several other vehicles for motivational communication.

Your Mission

Make sure the mission of your team remains a recurring theme in your leadership. If the mission is to become the best sales team in your market, or the best construction team, or the best accounting team, legal team, football team, auto repair shop or limousine service, stay focused on the plan to achieve your vision. When the team's vision for their mission grows dim, their motivation declines.

In addition to the team's mission, make sure your followers understand your approach to your mission in leadership. They need to know not only what goals you are leading them to achieve, but also what kind of a leader you want to be. Chandler and Richardson say, *"The more open we all are about how we intend to lead, the more motivated our people will be"* (Chandler and Richardson 2005, p. 196).

Ideas

When you communicate new ideas to your followers with convincing passion, you provide them with motivational adrenaline. The same is true when you encourage new ideas from them. New ideas stimulate the mind. Great ideas stimulate the spirit. Keep their creative juices flowing, and everyone will benefit.

Exchanging ideas not only encourages creativity and

problem solving, it can also help followers develop a better perspective. People often need help with their perspective. Sometimes the one they have just isn't working. One of the most important contributions motivational leaders provide is teaching people how to think. Not brainwashing them. Just offering them a different perspective when they've become discouraged, frustrated or bewildered. Help your followers find fresh ways to look at things, especially things which are new or which they don't understand.

Motivational leaders often hear these words from their followers: "I really appreciate this conversation. You've given me a whole new way of looking at this, and now I feel good about it." Turning a follower around from the attitude, "Take this away from me" to "Bring it on!" is a thrilling and rewarding achievement for the leader as well as the follower.

Sometimes motivating an employee toward an attitude adjustment requires counseling techniques similar to those used in confrontation. But sometimes the employee just needs you to give them hope and purpose – a renewed desire to persevere. Sometimes it's just about reassurance and support.

Support

Your desire to support your followers must be communicated. Your communication style cannot be a "no news is good news" style. Nor can it be, "You still have a job don't you? That means I support you." Motivational leadership requires more.

It includes explanations of the kind of support you intend to provide. As mentioned before, let them know how you intend to lead.

It also includes reciprocal feedback. Your followers need to know where they stand with you, and you need to know where you stand with them. Express your appreciation and your disappointments. As we discussed earlier when discussing a shortfall, maintain the employee's dignity, but let him know what you were expecting from him, the fact that he fell short, and what he needs to do to meet your expectations in the future. Expressing disappointment is as valuable support as expressing appreciation, as long as it ends with the desire to improve.

Communication also includes listening, and listening demands response. With all that is said about the importance of listening, much less is said about the importance of responding. The quality of your response demonstrates the quality of your listening. When you respond thoughtfully, sincerely and sensitively, you show your appreciation of the other person, and you show that you have truly listened to her.

Another important way a leader provides support is through encouragement and reassurance. We are not talking about giving a false sense of security. If one is in trouble he needs to know it. When employees are down, you need to reassure them that you still believe in them, even as you counsel them on steps they must take to get back on track.

If an employee is in a difficult situation, reassure him that his perseverance will pay off, and that even during the period of tribulation he is developing new strengths that will benefit him for the rest of his life. If the situation is extremely difficult suggest, "If you can hang in there and draw on your 'whatever it takes' attitude, this will provide some of your proudest stories for years to come. It's the kind of situation that creates long-term success." Encourage him with the reasons you believe he has what it takes to succeed.

One of the most practical ways to provide supportive communication is by helping your followers to find solutions to their challenges. Even as you are training them to figure out solutions, begin by telling what you would do if you were in their situation. If you don't know because it's a situation that you've never experienced or successfully mastered, find someone else who has mastered it, or at least experienced it. Your employee will appreciate that you cared enough to go to the trouble, and you will have learned something valuable yourself for the future. If you do not have time to pursue this avenue, direct them to the resource so they can pursue it on their own.

Standards and Expectations

Make sure the standards you have set for your team are clearly and consistently communicated. Don't expect your followers to absorb them by osmosis. Standards need to be put into words. In some cases they need to be put into numbers – as with measurable goals or measurable performance standards. The clearer your standards are, the more motivating they will be; the more vague, the less motivating. Be sure every member of your team understands your standards, and resolve any disagreements or anxieties over your standards. Enforce the standards consistently. And make sure you demonstrate your own passion for upholding the standards yourself.

Communicate what your followers can expect to happen. Describe the results you expect if everyone does what they're supposed to, and what results you expect if they don't. Point out external variables that could affect the results, but explain them in a way that is realistic without sounding like you're making excuses. Your spirit in setting these expectations sounds like this: "Here's what we're going to do. Here's how we're going to do it. Here's what we hope will be the result. Here's how everyone will benefit from that result if it is achieved."

Your followers should understand that they are committing not only to the goals and standards, but also to each other.

Communication During Change

During times of change communication is more important than ever. When a team goes through a period of change in management, policy, strategy or structure – or if it is going through a period of innovation – the way the change is communicated is an important factor in its success. If your team believes in the change they can make it succeed. If they do not believe in it or understand its purpose, the risk of failure increases.

Obviously change is intended for good, and yet when it is not explained clearly or respectfully, it can be perceived negatively. Usually, if the vision is articulated and the benefits of the change spelled out to those who will be shouldering the burden, it will be embraced. It seems so easy, and yet this vital piece of the puzzle is often left out, so employees must interpret the change for themselves. Worse still, they question the reason the change was not communicated.

For example, if a new manager is hired, employees may wonder, "Why was she chosen? What is her vision? In what ways will we be better off with her than we were before?" The sooner and more clearly this information is communicated, the more confident the employees will be in the decision, and the more easily the new manager will be accepted.

With changes in strategy or policy, providing answers to similar questions can help employees embrace the change more enthusiastically. Why will the new way be better than the old way? How does the change fit into the bigger picture of the company's vision and direction? The more confusing or threatening the change may be perceived, the more important it is to articulate the vision, purpose and benefits of the change.

Communication is an important element of innovation. Research, inspiration and teamwork produce innovations which can take an entire organization to its next level. If the innovation is not communicated properly to employees, the potential of the innovation can be squandered, along with all the effort it took to bring the innovation to life. On the other hand, effective communication can propel the innovation to its full potential. Let employees know how the idea was born, what need it was designed to fulfill, the process by which it was created, the plan for its implementation, and the vision for its success. For innovation, and for change in general, communication that is complete, respectful and enthusiastic will help your team to maximize the opportunities of the new direction, and will win more support for your leadership at the same time.

Communicate for Resolution

While cell phones and e-mail enable us to communicate more quickly and frequently, employees continue to bemoan the need for better communication. If we can communicate information more efficiently than ever before, why aren't we solving the problem? Because the greatest triumph of communication is not to convey information, but to achieve resolution. Information is the path, while resolution is the destination. Your communication will be most effective when the goal of resolution stays in focus.

Consistency

Consistency is a characteristic of motivational leadership that has not received the attention it deserves. It seems to have gotten lost amidst our fascination with the virtues of spontaneity, flexibility, adaptability and innovation. We can maintain our respect for all of these fine qualities and still focus on the motivational value of consistency. Unfortunately, consistency is sometimes misfiled under the headings of stodginess, complacency, or a non-progressive commitment to maintaining the status quo. This is a big mistake. Consistency is entirely compatible with spontaneity, creativity, innovation and change.

Consistency is important for upholding the standards you have set, and enforcing them in a way that supports the value system you have defined. Followers see consistency as an important virtue in the kind of leader they want to follow. They see it as reliable and trustworthy. Inconsistency erodes trust and looks weak.

To create an environment of motivation through high standards, you want to avoid the kinds of inconsistencies which could cause a follower to make any of the following statements:

- "The rules keep changing from day to day."
- "We never know if we're doing the right thing or not."

- "What good is having a policy when you never know if it's going to be enforced?"
- "If it had been someone else instead of me, the answer would have been yes."
- "If I'm going to persuade the boss to do it my way, I need to wait until he's in a better mood."

Your followers need to see in your leadership style the kind of consistency that implies stability and trustworthiness. It may sound mundane for a leader to be predictable, but predictability gives followers a sense of security.

Here is the way followers need to see consistency in your leadership.

- You believe the same thing from one day to the next.
- The information and direction you give them is reliable.
- You will stand behind them if they do what you tell them.
- You are decisive. Even if you cannot make a decision on the spot, you tell them when you will get them an answer, and then you meet the deadline you set.
- You enforce your standards consistently and impartially.
- You don't cave in on a principle in order to avoid a difficult situation. (Of course there are times when an exception is truly the right thing to do, but that's different than making an exception because it's the path of least resistance.)

While you need to enforce your standards and policies consistently, this does not mean you have to treat everyone the same. If you have an employee who acts more responsibly, it's okay to give her more responsibility. If someone has earned a higher level of trust over a period of time, you can give him more latitude in ways that do not violate the basic job description to which everyone else must adhere. If someone has proven herself to be more self-sufficient, you can allow her a corresponding increase in autonomy. It's okay for people to earn privileges. There's nothing unfair about that. The reasoning, principles and values behind your decisions still remain consistent.

Follow Through

Willingness to follow through is another important standard by which your followers will evaluate your leadership. Follow through is important to your reputation because it is a symbol of your credibility. Unfortunately, many leaders don't realize its importance. They let it slide because they get distracted.

Follow through is simple:
1. Finish what you start.
2. Do what you say you will do when you say you will do it.

Many managers simply forget what an important a role these two fundamental principles play in motivational leadership. They let their commitments (follow through is an issue of commitment) slip through the cracks because they have other priorities that seem more urgent. They decide that their follow through can wait. Then each day the commitment they have neglected grows less important.

The truth is this simple: leaders who stay focused on these two principles for follow through build credibility. In fact, failure to follow through is one of the foremost grievances employees today express against their managers in corporate culture surveys.

Following the next steps will ensure your reputation as a trustworthy leader.

Treat Follow Through As a Commitment.

Think of follow through as more than just an item on your to do list that is subject to revision as other demands on your time arise. Think of it instead as a serious commitment – a matter of integrity that will significantly affect the motivation of your team, and their trust in you. Follow through is the measure of your credibility that is easiest for your followers to identify. It is important to your followers' motivation because it demonstrates how much you respect, appreciate and value them. It tells them where they rank on your list of priorities. Your ability to follow through – to do what you say you will do – represents your commitment to your team, which in turn will help shape the standards to which they commit themselves.

Make Commitments Carefully.

One reason managers have a hard time with follow through is that they overcommit themselves. They promise to follow through on more items than they possibly can. Why does this happen? Usually it is for one of two reasons. The first is that it's easier to say yes than no. The second is that they don't think through the tasks to which they commit.

The purpose of a commitment is not to put a smile on the employee's face, or to get them off your back. It is to provide support and establish trust. If you can't honor the commitment, you will wind up with a worse relationship, and a worse reputation, than if you had said no in the first place.

Think all the way through a task before you commit to it. How many factors are involved? How many other people will be involved? How many other commitments do you have, and how many more can you anticipate before you have fulfilled the one you are about to make? Are you sure you will be able to follow this all the way through by the deadline to which you have agreed?

Making a commitment includes setting the right expectations. Tell the employee when you will get their issue resolved. If relevant, tell them how you will get it resolved. Then follow through in the time period to which you committed. Don't overpromise, but don't hedge unnecessarily. Don't rely on a time cushion you don't really need. It will wind up making it harder for you to follow through on some other commitment later. Just tell the employee how soon you can do it. It's perfectly all right to tell him you have other commitments you need to honor first.

What about deadlines? If you commit to a deadline, aren't you painting yourself into a corner? Why not just tell the employee you'll get to it as soon as you can? Because commitments without deadlines often wind up as empty promises. A deadline is just as important to the commitment as the task itself. You will also be asking for timely commitments from them, and they will feel more respected and more motivated by an environment of mutual accountability.

No leader has time to accommodate all requests. Your employees know that. When you cannot accommodate a request, go ahead and say so. It may be a fleeting or unnecessary request anyway. Or it may be a request for you to do something that they should be doing themselves. Let's talk about that next.

Let Your Followers Do Their Part.

Some employees slip easily into a habit of calling their bosses with every need that pops into their head, like a reflex. They don't stop to think how serious the need is, or if they could take care of it themselves. It's just easier for them to call you than to think it through. You cannot afford to let these employees disrupt your schedule. Don't agree to solve a problem for them just because you can take care of it yourself faster than you can teach them how to do it.

Self-sufficiency is one of the great gifts a leader can give followers. It's the truth of the old saying about giving a person a fish or teaching him how to fish for himself. One of your most valuable time management tools is the ability to turn some of your followers' requests back to them. Any time an employee asks you to shoulder a responsibility that could be theirs, take that opportunity to show them how to become more self-sufficient. The time it takes to teach them to solve the problem for themselves will pay greater time management dividends for you. By taking the time to teach your employees how to overcome more of their own challenges, you will free up time to follow through on issues that do require your attention. At the same time, your employees' feelings of self-sufficiency will increase their motivation. Self-sufficiency is one more indication of a team with high standards.

Now let's take a closer look at how empowerment works, and how to teach your followers to become more self-sufficient. This will enable you to focus on being a motivational leader instead of a full-time firefighter.

Motivation From the Heart

CHAPTER 7

DIRECTION AND EMPOWERMENT

Most people feel motivated when they feel empowered. As a leader, you can increase your followers' motivation by empowering them to take initiative in those responsibilities and decisions which can increase their success. When you empower your followers with more responsibility and authority, you increase their self-confidence and help them to become self-sufficient. One of the greatest gifts that motivational leaders can give their followers is self-sufficiency. The more self-sufficient they become, the better they feel about themselves. As their self-esteem improves, so does their performance, which in turn builds their self-esteem even further. It is an energy that perpetuates itself. In leadership, the primary goal of empowerment is to teach your followers to take initiative and become self-sufficient. Empowerment enables employees to motivate themselves.

This growth in your followers also produces a wonderful side effect: they respect you more as a leader. People want to follow a leader who empowers them. When you help them feel better about themselves, they will feel better about you. This is the nature of leadership. So empowerment is another great way to energize and motivate your followers, increase their self-confidence, and increase their loyalty to you.

Self-sufficiency and motivation go hand in hand. The more self-sufficient your followers become, the greater will be their belief in themselves and in their purpose, and their desire to improve will increase. This motivation leads to greater self-sufficiency. Self-sufficiency comes from empowerment, and empowerment comes from direction. Now let's see how all this works.

Bruce and Pepitone make the following points about empowerment.

"*Managers often think in terms of giving their employees motivation. But that's not what you should give your employees if you want them to be motivated. Instead, broadly speaking, you need to give them:*
- *the responsibility for achieving something, and*
- *the authority to do it their own way.*

"*This* **empowerment** *unleashes tremendous energy and motivation. When you give your employees responsibility and authority together, they feel that you trust them and value them*" (Bruce and Pepitone 1999, p. 60).

Empowerment is a concept that many organizations want to embrace, but few actually do, often because they don't know where to start. One of the great misconceptions about empowerment is that it begins by giving people power – by giving them more authority over the tasks for which they are responsible. But that is not where you start. Empowerment does not begin with giving power. It begins with giving direction. Then it evolves into giving more responsibility. Then it evolves further into a higher level of self-sufficiency. Empowerment is an evolving process, and the first stage is direction.

We often think of giving direction as telling someone what to do. But then how does giving direction help to empower people? The kind of direction that leads to empowerment requires a six-step process. Telling what to do is only the first step. So let's go through each of the six steps.

1. Here's what to do.

Make sure your initial instruction is clear. There should be no doubt in the follower's mind about exactly what you want them to do. The goal needs to be specific. They need to understand your definition of a successful outcome. See where they stand on the issue. Are they buying in to what you are asking them to do? Do they see any problem in achieving their objective? Help them get started, and make sure they do get started.

Here's an example. You are an upper level manager, and you supervise a recently promoted middle level manager named Rachel. Rachel supervises Robert, who has become a challenge. He is not meeting his goals, and he has developed a negative attitude. You get word back that Robert is voicing his negativity to other members of his team. You need for Rachel to resolve the issue. You say, "Rachel, I need you to talk with Robert to help him get back on track. What is your take on his whole situation?"

She responds, "I have to admit, I've been starting to wonder about it myself."

You: "It's not just his performance. It's also his attitude, and now he's starting to bring other people down, too. Are you aware of that?"

Rachel: "Yes, I've heard a few rumblings lately."

You: "Okay. Then I need for you to get this resolved very soon. Can you do that?"

Rachel: "I think so."

You: "Do you have any concerns about it?"

Rachel: "Well, I think he's just going through some personal stuff right now. I'm pretty sure it'll all work itself out, and then he'll be fine. In the meantime, I don't want to make him paranoid. If I hassle him about it, he may just get worse. He's always been a good employee. I don't want him to feel like we're not supporting him."

If you had stopped when Rachel said, "I think so," the conversation would not have gone far enough. You know from experience that you are asking Rachel to do something difficult, and you know this will be the first time she will be confronting an employee about his performance. After you tell her what she needs to do, ask for feedback. Make sure she understands that you are not just asking her to talk to Robert, you are asking her to help him improve. Her conversation with Robert will not complete the mission. Robert's improvement will complete the mission. You now realize that Rachel will need more direction in order to complete her mission successfully.

2. Here's how to do it.

The main reason Rachel is not yet comfortable with the task is that she is not fully confident that she knows what to do, or what to expect. She doesn't seem to be sure that confronting Robert is even the right thing to do. Step 3 in our process is why to do it, and there will be times when Step 3 needs to come before Step 2. For now we will talk about how first, and then why.

Go ahead and walk Rachel through it, along the lines of what we explained in Chapter Six in the section on confrontation. You know both Rachel and Robert, so your suggestions can be specific as well as general. What Rachel really wants to know is, "How would you do it?" Start with that. You could role play, with Rachel playing Robert, if you feel that would help her.

You are preparing Rachel in a way that will increase her confidence. Talk it all the way through, anticipating possible negative reactions from Robert as well as positive ones. You want Rachel to be in a position where she can walk into the situation feeling, "However Robert responds, I'll know what to do." (Or at least, "However he responds, I'll be fine.")

Another benefit of your conversation with Rachel is that she will know what approach you support. This way she knows that if she takes the approach you discuss, you will back her up if the need arises.

Give Rachel reassurance that everything will be fine. Help her envision the happy ending: Robert will, immediately or eventually, feel grateful that she talked with him. Help her envision Robert respecting her because she handled this difficult situation respectfully and compassionately, yet firmly. After all, she is helping Robert to achieve a higher level of excellence in his results and his perspective. Help her also to envision a more motivated team without Robert's negative influence. Finally, help her to envision the satisfaction she will have with herself once she has completed her mission and expanded her comfort zone. She will become a more accomplished manager as a result of the conversation she is about to have.

3. Here's why to do it that way.

Rachel needs to know how to conduct her conversation with Robert, but she also needs to know why it is important. Her initial response implied she believed that given time, the situation would take care of itself. You can motivate her to embrace the challenge by instilling a sense of purpose in the mission to help Robert improve his attitude, behavior and performance. Help her to understand the benefits her conversation with Robert can produce.

She will be giving Robert an opportunity to improve and coaching him on how to do it. Robert can become successful, and a good influence and a source of positive energy to his co-workers. If he is interested in improving, then he will be grateful. If he is not, that will become apparent soon enough. At that point, it can be addressed as refusing to improve after he was given the opportunity.

Rachel will be using the same six-step process with Robert that you use with her. The approach to direction and empowerment we are describing here applies at every level of your organization.

Rachel needs to understand that this situation is also a defining moment for her as a leader. What kind of a leader does she really want to be? What kind of reputation does she want to have as a leader? Will she provide strong leadership when it is needed in order to uphold the standards of the team? As her mentor, you have an important opportunity to help her achieve a breakthrough in her own leadership ability.

She has an opportunity to build her confidence by stepping outside of her comfort zone and expanding it.

She has an opportunity to increase the motivation of her team by removing influences which threaten its motivation.

And what if she lets this opportunity go by? And then the next opportunity after this? What kind of a leader will she become if she makes the wrong choice at this fork in the road? Will she eventually be perceived as a weak, dispassionate leader who only looks after Number One? What happens to the standards of her team? What happens to Robert? Does he just keep sinking, and start dragging others down with him? All of these questions stress the importance of explaining "why" as well as "how." You are teaching her not only techniques, but also a thought process for strong, motivational leadership.

There is one more reason Rachel's conversation with Robert is important. She will show Robert that she leads with compassion. She will meet with Robert because she respects him and is committed to doing her part to help him be successful. She doesn't have to put herself through this. She could just write him up and try to motivate him by fear. Instead she demonstrates that she doesn't just motivate through fear and authority; she motivates from the heart. That's the kind of leader that people want to follow.

4. *Will you do it? When?*

This is the stage that so often slips through the cracks. Many managers who are committed to giving good direction – who do their very best with the first three steps in order to empower their employees with the skill and confidence to accomplish their mission – forget to close the loop. They don't close the deal. Once the first three steps are accomplished – the employee knows what to do, how to do it and why it's so important – there may still be dangling issues to address before the employee can complete the task successfully.

You will close the loop with Rachel by making sure you know where she stands on the following questions. The answers may already be obvious from your discussion, but if they are not, this is the time to resolve them. You are about to send her into action, and soon she will be at the point of no return.

- **Can you do it?** Do you feel you are truly capable of doing it? Are you comfortable enough to do it? Do you feel that you will be successful? Is there anything you don't feel confident about? Are you ready to go?
- **Do you feel that it's the right thing to do?** Is there anything about the action you are about to take that feels wrong, or is not up to your standards, or is not consistent with your personal values?
- **Are you willing to do it?** Is there anything that will stop you? Do you have any reservations that we have not resolved? Are you committing to me that you will truly do this?
- **When will you do it?** As we have discussed before, this kind of commitment is incomplete without a deadline.

Your goal is for Rachel to be able to attack her mission with as much motivation – as much belief in herself and her purpose – as possible. She needs to commit to you *when* she will do it. She does not have to feel 100% tranquil, especially if it's a challenging task that she's never tackled before, but she needs to be ready.

5. *Call me after you've done it and tell me how it went.*

Now we're beginning to make the transition from direction into empowerment. The direction phase has been completed, but you're not done yet. You have two more steps in order for your direction to evolve into empowerment and self-sufficiency.

Ask Rachel to call you soon after she has had her conversation with Robert so the two of you can debrief. How did it go? How did Robert respond? How did it end? Do you feel good about the way it turned out? Do you feel good about the way you handled it? If you had it to do over, is there anything you would do differently? Did I give you any bad advice? (You are looking for opportunities to improve as well.) Did you and Robert agree on a plan for his improvement? What kind of a commitment did he give you? What is your next step with Robert? How do you feel it will go with Robert from this point on? How are *you* doing? Are you glad you did it?

This is a critical step in the empowerment process. It gives you and Rachel an opportunity to evaluate your progress together. It takes the two of you to the next level of accountability. You can each decide whether your direction to her was effective, and whether you are satisfied with the results. She can tell you whether she believes she has grown.

There is one more benefit to this step. Anticipating this joint evaluation of her efforts will give Rachel one more source of purpose about achieving resolution with Robert.

6. Can you do it by yourself next time?

Now comes the ultimate purpose of this whole process. Is Rachel able and willing to handle this kind of situation by herself next time? If she's not entirely confident yet, you may have to help her a few more times. Self-sufficiency is not always an overnight process. It develops over time.

It may get to the point where you have to throw her out of the nest. "Rachel, you need to be able to handle this situation by yourself. I've taught you all I know. The rest is up to you. With this kind of challenge, you're on your own now."

The purpose of this six-step process is to give your followers direction in a way that empowers. You are not giving them power. You are preparing them to take the torch from you naturally. All of a sudden they are empowered. They are more self-sufficient. They communicate good ideas more openly and passionately, because they have more confidence in their thoughts as well as their skills. They can handle problems, decisions and strategies by themselves, and you now have more time to devote to other parts of your leadership mission.

* * *

Here are a few footnotes on ways to help your followers become more self-sufficient.

Explain your ideas of empowerment to the team, and let these ideas be a continuing theme of your leadership. Help them understand the concept of empowerment and its purpose of giving everyone more control over their day-to-day challenges. Then reinforce your message one on one as necessary, as shown in the example of Rachel and Robert.

One of the goals of self-sufficiency is to enable your followers to solve their own problems. Whenever an employee brings you a problem, ask them to bring you a proposed solution as well. This will soon become a habit that will make employees more self-sufficient as they develop motivation for solving their own problems. Over time it will increase self-confidence and strengthen mutual respect and trust.

Direction and Empowerment

Discourage employees from bringing you the same problem again and again. After awhile, it becomes manipulative. The purpose of your six-step process is to eliminate this kind of dependence. Motivation requires the desire to improve. Don't let your employees succumb to feelings of helplessness. Show your confidence that they are bigger than their challenges.

Explain that if they are willing to take more initiative to resolve their own challenges, it will free you up to provide better service in other ways that will benefit them even more.

Once the concept of empowerment begins to take hold, its natural course is to gain momentum. Self-confidence and motivation continue to increase with the successes of self-sufficiency. Our next chapter will explain more ways to increase the self-confidence of those who follow you.

Motivation From the Heart

Part Three

TEACHING ATTITUDES FOR SUCCESS

CHAPTER 8

BUILDING YOUR TEAM'S SELF-CONFIDENCE

Where to Start

One reason some people are more motivated than others is that they have a more confident self-definition. They see themselves as being capable of success and worthy of it. People with weaker self-definitions wrestle with questions of whether they have the ability to succeed and whether they truly deserve success. They define themselves as second-rate. This self-definition becomes their comfort zone.

You can make a difference here. Leaders can wield a dramatic influence on the self-image of their followers. You can help followers with a weaker self-image to become more motivated by helping them to improve their self-definitions. You can help them to break through the barrier of their self-limiting comfort zone.

In Chapter Three, when we discussed "Belief in Self," we suggested you could help your followers improve their self-definitions by telling them what good attributes you see in them and why you believe in them. The more specific you can be, the more powerful an impact you will have. Our self-definition improves when we feel appreciated. When we discussed the Pygmalion Effect, we saw that the more your followers respect you, the more influence you will have in helping them to improve their self-definitions.

When people feel confident in themselves, they feel clear-headed and purposeful. When they lose self-confidence, demons can surface: self-doubt, cynicism, hopelessness, fear that things will go wrong, fear of being undermined by others – the variety of feelings that drag people down and cause them to fail simply because they're not able to produce their best effort. Leaders help followers to clear their heads, revitalize their purpose and conquer the demons that can thwart their success.

Give your followers opportunities to stretch in ways that will improve their self-definition when they succeed – a challenge slightly more difficult than their last success, a little more responsibility than they've had up to this point. Provide your support by showing that you truly believe they will succeed, and why you believe it. These are the successes that help them break down the self-limiting barriers that clutter their minds.

Now let's dig a little deeper into why people have self-limiting thoughts. If you can understand what causes them, you can help your followers conquer them. Here is a list of a number of factors that contribute to self-limiting self-definitions. Our list will include some challenges we

have already discussed, along with some new ones we will tackle throughout the rest of this chapter.
1. Lack of belief in self.
2. Lack of belief in purpose.
3. A self-definition defined more by what one is not than by what one is.

    Examples would be, "I'm not a public speaker"…"I'm not a natural extrovert"…"I don't have an aggressive personality."

    Encourage employees to define themselves in terms of who they are. Also don't allow them to use "what I'm not" as a reason to avoid an endeavor they should pursue.
4. Defining self more in terms of weaknesses than strengths.

    Examples of this would be, "My parents didn't raise me to have high self-esteem"…"I never have been very good at asking for things."

    Your people need to love their strengths, and seek out ways to use them more.
5. Lack of passion.
6. Lack of vision.
7. Lack of knowledge or understanding.
8. Feelings of helplessness, frustration or futility.

    Examples: "I'll never have the opportunity to grow with this company because my boss is too insecure"…"I'm not appreciated here"…"There's just no market for what I'm selling."

    Encourage employees to understand that current circumstances are not the end of the story, but are leading somewhere. Also be aware that employees may compromise their standards if they feel

unvalued by others.
9. Blaming bad luck.
   Cynical feelings may cause some people to think, "Whoever said life is supposed to be fair?" However, they often confuse fairness with instant gratification. We all need to give fairness time to complete its process. There are many pieces to the fairness puzzle, some of which we don't understand until later.
10. Feelings of not being respected or believed in by others.
11. Feelings of not being supported.
    Example: "I've been hung out to dry."
    Seize the opportunity to show how self-sufficient you can be when you're not getting the support you think you deserve. Encourage your employees to embrace this attitude as well.
12. Feelings that you (or your efforts) don't matter.
    Focus on the ways you do have impact, not on the ways you don't. As a leader, you will greatly influence your followers' perception of their value. This is another area where you lead by example so that your followers will be motivated to emulate you. They can have a positive influence on each other.
13. Feelings that other people are better than you.
14. Pessimism.
15. Lack of will.
16. Lack of discipline.
17. Lack of perseverance. (The lack of a "What will it take?" mentality.)
18. Unwillingness to step out of your comfort zone.

19. Fear of failure.
20. Fear of success.
    We will explain what we mean by "fear of success" and how to overcome it later in this chapter.
21. Fear of conflict.
22. Fear of attention.
    "I prefer to fly under the radar."
    Providing a positive influence to others is one of the most important contributions people can make in life. Encourage employees not to let their fear of attention cause them to forfeit this opportunity.
23. Fear of embarrassment.
    "I'll never get over it."
    Yes you will.

Identifying these factors that contribute to self-limiting self-definitions in yourself and your followers empowers you both to begin creating stronger self-definitions. Now that you are aware of these self-defeating attitudes, you can consciously work on developing new attitudes which are the opposite. These new attitudes will lead to stronger self-definitions. As self-definitions improve, so does self-confidence. In fact, a strong self-definition creates self-confidence in situations where the natural tendency is to feel inadequate.

We have talked briefly in previous chapters about how you can motivate your followers through encouragement and reassurance. Now let's see how encouragement and reassurance can improve confidence as well as motivation. Then we will discuss how to help overcome self-doubt, conquer fear, and increase self-discipline. While discussing those topics, we will also address the self-limiting attitudes we listed above.

Providing Encouragement and Reassurance

Do you know anyone who radiates an encouraging and reassuring demeanor? Being in their presence makes you feel better about your situation and about yourself. They seem to do it so easily and naturally. That is because they are genuine and sincere. They genuinely care about the well-being of others. They are sincerely interested in people. They listen carefully and respond thoughtfully. They are unselfish. They believe in others, and they want others to believe in themselves. They seem to have a real sense of purpose about giving joy and energy to the world around them. They seek to enrich people's lives. When they are leaders, people want to follow them. They give what people want from a leader.

One definition of "encourage" in Webster's New World Dictionary is "to give courage, hope or confidence to." Of course, encouragement should be about giving courage, but we rarely think of it that way. We think of encouragement more in terms of making people feel good. But in leadership, encouragement truly is about giving courage, hope and confidence to your followers.

The opposite is discouragement – taking your followers' courage away. When a parent discourages a child from trying to catch a stray raccoon that may have rabies, they want to take the child's courage away for that particular situation. But do you ever really want to take your followers' courage away from the pursuit of excellence? Unfortunately we see leaders discourage their followers' pursuit of excellence all the time. They don't mean to; they're just not thinking about the consequences of their approach. Instead:

- They just think they're making a joke, not realizing the power of ridicule. ("Hey Ralph, why don't you start out the training portion of our meeting by teaching the rest of us how to go three weeks without a sale.")
- They think they're shaping up the employee, when in fact they're tearing him down by conveying little confidence in his ability to succeed.
- They think they're providing support by handling an employee's adversity, when in fact they're implying he isn't up to the task, and there's no purpose in teaching him how to do it right.
- They think they're simply asking employees to step up to the plate by asking for longer hours, when in fact the employees have become exhausted from long hours and discouraged by the lack of results their grinding has produced.

Remember that as a leader your goal is to give courage, hope and confidence to your followers, not to take it away.

A Webster definition for reassurance is "to restore to confidence." Reassurance does not merely say, "Don't give up." It adds "...because I know you have what it takes, and once you prevail, it will all be worth it." Like encouragement, reassurance blesses your followers with courage, hope and confidence.

You are not only providing encouragement and reassurance to your followers, you are creating an environment that nurtures these precious resources. Show special appreciation to those employees who encourage and reassure their co-workers, especially when it relates to the shared purpose of your team.

To create this environment you will need to show the demeanor we have just described. You are creating an environment that helps people develop healthy self-definitions, so they will need to see that you have a healthy self-definition. If you appear as a whipped leader, where are their courage, hope and confidence supposed to come from? How will you be able to provide encouragement and reassurance to the team if you cannot provide it to yourself?

Reassure your followers that the leaders they follow have a vision with a viable plan, and confidence enough in that vision that they will pursue it with courage. Followers can become profoundly discouraged and fearful if confident leadership is missing.

Show that you are sincerely interested in them. Reassurance appears empty if it seems that you're not really interested in them except for the results they produce.

When you convey to a follower your confidence that they will succeed, and you explain the reasons why you believe they will succeed, it is like giving them a megadose of vitamin B-12. Remember the Pygmalion Effect. As their leader, you become an important frame of reference for measuring their success, and their potential for success. Your opinion of what they can accomplish becomes part of their self-definition. If their performance is not yet where it should be, help them to believe in what they can be. Why should they believe in themselves? Because you do!

You can encourage them even when you are counseling on underperformance. Let them know what they can do to become successful, and that you want to see them achieve that success. Encouragement and reassurance do not mean telling a person who is falling short of their potential, "You're fine the way you are." It means helping them to believe in themselves more than they currently do. It means guiding them toward success by saying, "You will be successful if you…"

When employees express discouragement, begin by validating their feelings. Validating their feelings is not the same as endorsing them. It is merely showing that you understand why they feel the way they do. It is better than saying, "You're stupid to feel that way." That would only make them feel worse about themselves.

Know when encouragement is appropriate and when it is demeaning. Be sensitive to distinguish between the right time to encourage, the right time to listen, and the right time to validate. If your first response to their discouragement is a pep talk, they might feel as though you are trivializing their problem. They are already frustrated, so their response to your attempts at encouragement may be, "He just doesn't get it." They may feel as though you don't really care, and you just want to get them off your back.

By validating feelings, you are showing respect, showing that you take them seriously, and taking the first step toward helping to develop a more appropriate perspective for handling whatever is discouraging. When a pep talk is the appropriate solution, it can still follow validation.

Sometimes the best way to encourage is to listen. Let the employee process verbally. Often they will harness their negativity by themselves. Just stay focused on helping them clear away the mental clutter, and the encouragement may take care if itself. They may walk away refreshed, saying to you, "Thank you for listening. That really helped me to sort through things." It is quite a compliment when someone says, "One thing I admire about you is that you're such a good listener." Listening shouldn't be that hard, yet it is considered a rare and precious virtue among leaders.

If you feel that their state is fragile, and yet you want to offer a different perspective gently and respectfully, you could say this: "What you're saying is legitimate and makes a lot of sense. Are you open to another perspective on how to think about it?"

Recognition and appreciation are among the most widely accepted forms of encouragement. However, don't praise people when they don't deserve it just to pump them up. This does not work because it's insincere. Showing that you care carries more weight than praise for someone who is profoundly discouraged.

Telling them what you or others admire about them can remind them of the person they were created to be, and that they have the ability to be that person whenever they earnestly desire it. Help them to understand the positive influence they could have, and the superior reputation they could create, as soon as they want to. Help them to see that they *do* matter, and that they *can* make a difference. The source of much of our discouragement comes from the belief that we don't matter. The first person who reminds us that we can make a difference – that we can offer positive influence which can improve the lives of others – is often the person who has the most profound influence on us. Great leaders realize they have this influence when followers tell them something like this:

- "You were the first person who ever believed in me."

- "I want to prove to you that I can be the person you think I am."
- "You've helped me see myself in a whole new way."
- "You have caused me to reach farther than I ever wanted to, because you helped me see the point of it."
- "You caused me to have dreams for myself that I never dared to dream on my own, and you made me want to live those dreams."
- Or, as Jack Nicholson said in the movie, *As Good As It Gets,* "You make me want to be a better man."

Don't try to encourage an employee by telling him he is on the fast track if he is not. You are setting up future discouragement that will be greater than the encouragement you are trying to provide. This approach to encouragement is different from helping people to believe in themselves. When a person tells you they want to be on the fast track, they may be telling you they are looking for a shortcut. Don't be lured in by the fact that they are "motivated to achieve success." People who are motivated want to do a better job. They want to *earn* a faster track, not demand one. They pursue mastery and let success, wealth, prestige and promotions be the result. The best kind of encouragement you can provide is letting them know that if they pursue excellence, their success will take care of itself, and they will find the right track at the right time.

Overcoming Self-Doubt

The battle between self-confidence and self-doubt occurs at a life-changing crossroads on our journey toward fulfilling our potential. How can you help those who follow you to win this battle?

First, you can help them understand it. Second, you can help them learn how to win it. Third, you can avoid indulging it. Now let's look at how to accomplish this.

To help your followers understand and win the battle against self-doubt, teach them that conquering self-doubt is a process that involves the following three steps.

1. Identify self-doubt as an enemy that must be conquered.

Conquering self-doubt begins by recognizing it. Self-doubt breaks into your mind in the same way a burglar breaks into a home. Like the burglar, self-doubt is a thief, trying to steal your courage, confidence and success. You may be asleep when the burglar breaks in, so you could not prevent it from happening. But this burglar makes a lot of noise to alert you. You may not be able to prevent self-doubt from breaking into your mind, but when it makes noise that disturbs your clarity and sense of purpose, you can catch it in the act.

You may think it is dangerous to try to stop a burglar, but the burglar of self-doubt is unarmed. You have the weapons. You can stop self-doubt in its tracks and send it to jail. No matter how many times self-doubt gets out of jail and breaks into your home, you can catch it every time. Self-doubt is an enemy which absolutely must be stopped.

How do you recognize this enemy? As with the burglar, it's easy. You recognize it as an intruder in your mind that has no place there, just as the burglar has no place in your home. Its unwelcome noise clutters your brain with "negative self-talk" and "mental interference." Self-doubt is the enemy who tells you you're not good enough.

The only way self-doubt can prevail is if you just don't hate it enough. You let it stay. Sometimes you even invite it in. When you feel your self-confidence, your self-image, your self-definition under attack from this enemy, you need to recognize the enemy and destroy it in an absolute, winner-take-all conquest. Negotiate no peace treaties. Destroy it. Accept no terms but unconditional surrender. Conquering self-doubt is serious business.

2. Define self-doubt.

One reason we fail to destroy self-doubt is that we fail to define it.

Self-doubt is the belief that our failures are real and that our successes are flukes.

This enemy is not only menacing, it is also irrational. Why should our failures be more real than our successes? It doesn't make sense, but that's good news. Knowing that self-doubt is irrational makes it easier to conquer. It is merely a phantom – a figment of our imagination. Yet it is the kind of mental clutter that wreaks havoc if we don't stop it dead in its tracks.

How do successful people handle failure? They acknowledge it, but don't allow it to become part of their self-definition. In fact, successful people see failure as one of the most valuable stepping stones to success – part of the process of fulfilling their potential. The fact that they fail does not make them a failure. It simply means they have more work to do. But they will embrace that work, because they do what it takes to achieve their goals. This is a great example of the difference that perspective makes in our motivation and success.

3. Focus on the reasons you have been successful in the past.

Once you have identified self-doubt as an enemy to conquer, it is a very vulnerable enemy indeed. Now enjoy thinking about why you will succeed. What is it about you that has made you successful in the past? Each of us is uniquely gifted. Each of us has a unique genius. Each of us can succeed wherever we have true motivation: belief in ourselves, belief in our purpose, and the desire to improve every day.

The opposite of self-doubt is self-trust – trusting that your natural abilities combined with perseverance will enable you to succeed. Part of overcoming fear is trusting in yourself and in your innate abilities. Assume that the reason you were given a task is because others believed you could master it. If you do not trust yourself, then trust those who trust you.

It takes an act of conscious will to replace self-doubt with self-trust, and this act of will is one of the defining characteristics of a champion.

We perform at our highest level when we are in a relaxed, confident state. Self-trust is what enables us to relax enough to maximize our natural abilities, which are usually greater than we think they are.

As a leader with influence on your followers' self-definitions, you can help them to replace self-doubt with self-trust by learning about their past successes. Show your interest in learning their unique gifts and genius. Show your appreciation for these assets once you have discovered them. Help them apply their unique gifts and genius to the mission that lies before them.

If you want to help your followers to conquer self-doubt, you cannot afford to indulge it, and neither can they. Your followers must commit to join forces with you to conquer their enemy. Nothing less than total conquest is acceptable. If they continue to wallow in self-doubt – if they choose to give their self-doubt power to which it was never entitled, then you must confront them head on. Say to them, "You need to decide whether you will conquer self-doubt or let it conquer you. I can support you, but I can't fight your battle without you. When you've made your decision, let me know."

Conquering Fear

Suppose fear did not exist. Imagine what we could achieve! Nothing keeps us from fulfilling our destiny as much as fear. If we could conquer fear, we could finally become everything we were created to be. All of us would achieve the greatness that lies within us. Many people live out their whole lives without ever discovering their own greatness or achieving the success of which they are capable. Often fear is the enemy to whom they surrender. Fear is the big brother of self-doubt. As with self-doubt, conquering fear is a most important quest.

The ability to conquer fear is one of the characteristics of a champion. The ability to help followers conquer fear is a characteristic of a great leader. Helping your followers conquer fear begins with understanding it yourself. Let's look at how champions in any endeavor conquer fear. Then we'll use that understanding to help your followers become champions.

Fear Can Be Managed

Why can some people conquer fear while others are overpowered by it? How do some people seem to use fear as a springboard while others are dragged down by it? What does conquering fear really mean? How can you really make it happen, for yourself and for those who follow you?

Conquering fear does not mean eliminating it. It means learning how to manage it by transforming it from a negative force into a positive one. The first step in conquering fear is to appreciate that there are very few things we really need to fear. If we look back on our past fears, we realize that most of the time we were more afraid than we needed to be. Even those times when our fears were legitimate we survived. Often we even wound up better after the adversity was over than before it began. Champions thrive on the hope of unseen possibility during times of adversity.

As with self-doubt, champions conquer fear by first identifying it as an enemy. They realize that their reaction to fear is, in most situations, a choice. Once you develop a process for conquering fear, and then begin applying that process each day, you will find that conquering fear gets easier and easier. It creates an exciting new source of confidence.

We said that fear is the big brother of doubt. Doubt can attack an employee's performance – or even your own – much as it attacks an athlete's performance. Some experts consider doubt to be the primary cause of error in sports, even outranking lack of skill. We frequently see a less skilled athlete outperform a more skilled one because the less skilled athlete was more relaxed, confident and clearheaded on that particular day. We see a star athlete choke under pressure because on that one day he worried about losing instead of trusting his natural ability. As with athletes, doubt can inhibit the natural ability of the rest of us by cluttering our minds with visions of failure that can become self-fulfilling prophecies.

As a leader, your doubts and fears transmit themselves to your followers just as contagiously as your confidence, hope and courage do. Conquering your own fears and doubts not only unleashes your own natural ability, it also produces the kind of fearless confidence that helps you to inspire the best in your followers. Fearless confidence is not arrogant swagger. It is the comfortable self-assurance that helps your followers to feel that they are in the hands of a leader they can trust.

Escape Your Own Comfort Zone, Then Help Your Followers to Escape Theirs

One of the saddest consequences of fear is that it is so self-limiting. It imprisons you inside your comfort zone. In order to stay within the limits of your comfort zone, you must define yourself as being less than your true potential. When you stop defining yourself timidly and risk escaping your comfort zone, you discover that your comfort zone expands. As your comfort zone expands, so does your potential. Escaping the comfort zone prison begins momentum toward the highest level of success and fulfillment.

Conquering fear enables you to step out of your comfort zone. At the same time, stepping out of your comfort zone is one of the ways you learn to conquer fear. This cycle accelerates as you discover new ways to define yourself that are less self-limiting. From time to time you need to embrace challenges that seem difficult or uncomfortable in order to develop your strength, courage, confidence and energy. It's the kind of stretching that enables you to grow.

Now let's look at three examples of the kinds of fear your followers may have to confront. We will see how champions handle these fears. You can use their example to give your followers perspective on fear. The three fears we will examine will be:

- Fear of failure.
- Fear of success.
- Fear of change.

Fear of Failure

Champions are not afraid to fail. They don't want to fail, but they are not afraid to fail. This is a crucial distinction. We sometimes regard fear of failure as one of the greatest motivations of a true champion. But this explanation is oversimplified. A true champion's motivation is not simply the fear of failure. Their attitude may be, "Failure is not an option." Or it may be, "I will do whatever it takes to succeed, and I will do whatever it takes to avoid failure." But these are different ideas than merely the fear of failure. Fear of failure is a self-limiting emotion that must be overcome in order to achieve the highest level of championship over the long term.

Everyone fails. Often we are enriched by failure. We sometimes hear champions say, "I failed my way to success." They understand the concept that failures often lead to larger successes. Champions often credit previous failures more than previous successes for their ultimate successes over the long term. It is true that we grow more from our failures than from our successes.

The person looking for immediate gratification and the path of least resistance has every reason to fear failure. The champion looking for long-term growth has nothing to fear. Her successes lead to greatness in one way while her failures lead to it in another.

Fear of failure can be the self-limiting obstacle that prevents you from fulfilling your potential and achieving your goals. While fear of failure is natural, it needs to be managed correctly in order for you to keep growing. You can channel your fear of failure in a productive direction by cherishing the challenge you are facing for its future potential rather then dwelling on its current disappointment, frustration or embarrassment.

Don't allow the fear of making a mistake to make you afraid to take the action you need in order to be successful.

Suppose you feel immobilized by fear. How can you free yourself from that paralysis? One way is to ask yourself, "What would I do if I were not afraid?" This approach puts fear into its proper perspective in order for you to make the correct decision. It identifies fear as the self-limiting enemy of your potential, and gives you the opportunity to neutralize the fear so you can move forward. A similar approach would be to ask yourself, "If I knew there were no chance I could fail, what action would I take?" These two approaches may seem too easy to be effective, yet each of them opens up a whole new level of opportunities by making the conquest of fear so simple. Use these techniques to break free of the bondage of fear and self-limiting thinking.

Champions achieve success largely by transforming their fear of failure from a negative force into a positive one – from an enemy into a friend. They discover that success in the face of fear is often more satisfying than success in situations that produce no fear.

We all struggle with fear of failure to some extent. Embracing the challenge helps us conquer this fear. We achieve a higher level of self-confidence once we embrace the idea that even if we fail, we will succeed in greater ways later on.

When you do fail, let it go. Past failure does not imply future failure unless we allow it to. Many great success stories have a history of failure behind them. The most often-cited example is Abraham Lincoln. His failures in love, business and politics, along with personal challenges in his marriage and his melancholia, created in him the kind of courage, patience, perseverance, and wisdom to lead our nation through its most difficult years. In the business world, Harlan Sanders' setbacks ultimately resulted in the enormous success of Kentucky Fried Chicken, success which he claimed he never could have achieved without his failures. As with many scientists, the continuous failures of his thousands of experiments led Thomas Edison to his ultimate successes with electricity. The failures of these three men developed not only the character, but also the knowledge, skills and attitudes that produced their historic successes. Be sure you take something away from every failure that helps produce a future success.

Fear of Success

The reasons we fear failure seem obvious, but why would people fear success? Isn't success what everyone wants? The truth is that many people are more comfortable with failure than they are with success. Failure actually fits into their comfort zone more easily than success does. Many people do not reach the highest levels of success because they cannot envision themselves in that role. It is as though they do not believe that the role of champion is the one they were born to play. These feelings are rooted in fear. But what is there to be afraid of? Here are a few possibilities.

The more successful you become, the more competitive is your environment. People at your level are meeting a higher standard, and you are expected to meet that standard, too – all the time. So not only is the standard higher, the day-to-day expectations are higher.

Champions don't get the same sympathy losers get. It seems as though they are judged by different rules. When champions produce a result that is merely above average, they are often accused of being in a slump. Others performing at the same level are considered to be excelling. This new existence of competing at a higher level can sometimes feel frustrating and lonely.

Champions have to deal with the fact that others feel threatened by them. No one feels threatened by losers. No one is jealous of them. Losers are good people to have around because they make average performers feel like winners.

So the fear of success can be just as self-limiting as the fear of failure. In the middle lies mediocrity, which is the comfort level of most people. Average people can have a very comfortable existence. They won't be hassled. They will be allowed, and perhaps even encouraged, to remain mediocre, and that's fine with them. They don't want the responsibility of higher expectations. They don't want people asking, "What's wrong?" every time they don't win. They don't want the attention or accountability of being a champion. They want to earn a decent living with a minimum amount of pressure in the middle of the pack, flying below the radar.

People who are in the middle of the pack don't have to endure the humiliation of continuous failure or the jealousy from others that may result from continuous success. When people are in the middle, no one expects them to win or lose. There is never much at stake. Mediocrity can be a stable, comfortable existence.

Champions embrace opportunities to escape their comfort zones. They continue to redefine themselves at a higher level than their current one. They want to be held to a higher standard. To put it simply, champions are more comfortable winning, while losers are more comfortable losing.

Fear of success confines us to a self-limiting comfort zone. For some people, their comfort zone becomes a major part of their self-definition – their very identity. This identity may become one of the most important sources of their stability. Stepping outside of their comfort zone can literally threaten their stability, causing fear and anxiety. Some people feel more comfortable with a stable self-definition than they feel achieving the level of success that would threaten the stability of their self-definition. Surpassing their expectations of themselves (achieving a level of success that is greater than they expected) can threaten their self-definition, and thereby threaten their feelings of stability. Sometimes this sense of stability is more important to a person than their performance. Fear of success occurs when success threatens our comfort zone, our identity and our stability.

Many people create limiting self-definitions, and these definitions become boundaries across which they are afraid to step. That is the fear of success. Be aware that this is a very real syndrome. Take care you don't fall into it, and help your followers avoid this trap as well. Sometimes you will have to help them escape from the trap after they have gotten caught in it. Stepping outside of our comfort zone may seem threatening, but it is how "average people" grow into champions.

Escaping your comfort zone is how you grow, and growth should not produce instability. Growth should be a source of energy, motivation and opportunity. The ability to redefine ourselves is a good thing. It is one of the God-given gifts that only humans can enjoy. It's a shame to squander it.

How do champions overcome the fear of success? Much as they overcome any other fear. They begin by realizing that the fear itself is their own choice. After all, what is there to really fear? Is it the possibility that you are not truly worthy of the success, and now it will be taken away from you? You can't worry about that. You have to assume that if you were not capable of the success, you would not have achieved it in the first place. Now that you have achieved it, the issue is no longer ability. It now resides in the realm of the mental game. It is about the excitement of realizing that you do have championship ability, and that no one can take that away from you.

Championship ability does not mean that you will succeed every time. Champions lose. However, they manage their reaction to it, just as they also manage their reaction to winning. They don't self-destruct. They believe that they are not only worthy of success, but they were created for it.

When a champion's performance slips, she does not get discouraged. She refocuses to achieve her former level of excellence. Champions get back up after they fall, because they are not afraid to get back up.

Everyone has championship qualities within them. Champions are the ones who let these qualities blossom. They think of themselves as champions *before* they become champions. They are not afraid to think this way.

Champions *enjoy* success. They embrace it. They are thankful for it. Most of all, they are comfortable with it. They trust themselves. They identify self-doubt as the enemy and subdue it. Instead of asking, "Can I be successful?" they ask, "What will it take to be successful?" Then, once they achieve the higher standard they have set for themselves, they thrive on maintaining it.

Fear of Change

Why do we so often choose to believe that change will be bad? Why would we not choose to believe it will be good? If we choose to believe that change will be good, we position ourselves mentally to take advantage of its positive potential. We can also handle the downside of change with a better perspective. We will be able to see negative aspects of change in the larger context of its positive opportunities. Champions seek out the good in bad situations while others focus on the negative aspects of good situations.

Perspective is a huge factor in adapting to change. Once again we find ourselves in the arena of self-fulfilling prophecies. And once again we see fear as a choice. Change benefits champions much more often than it hurts them. However, sometimes change can hurt those who resist it. Resisting change can deprive us of opportunities. It can prevent us from expanding our reach. It can give us a reputation as someone who is afraid or unwilling to try new things. Position yourself so that you wind up stronger after the change instead of weaker.

Most change does not occur for the purpose of making things worse. There may be bumps or misfires along the way, but change usually occurs because there is a need for it. Those who embrace it are more likely to benefit from its positive potential. They may also be rewarded for their positive attitude in embracing the change while others are resisting it. Position yourself to maximize the opportunities of change by approaching it with a positive attitude.

Start out with an open mind and try to understand the change. People often reject change without even trying to understand it. Why did the change occur? What is the vision behind the change?

Change is one more example of stepping out of your comfort zone. Yes, it takes courage, but you can enjoy the courage and energy that stepping out of your comfort zone can provide. Life is a series of adventures, with each adventure setting up the next one. Change is part of that adventure.

Conquering Fear Requires a Sense of Purpose

Here are fourteen ideas to teach your followers that will help them manage their fears more productively. You not only want to help them conquer fear, you want to give them a strong sense of purpose about it.

1. Fear is self-limiting. Conquering fear will open the vault to many of your other abilities, enabling you to make the most out of each opportunity that comes your way.
2. Most of the time, fear is a choice.

3. Conquering fear does not mean eliminating it. It means learning how to manage it by transforming it from a negative force into a positive one.
4. When you feel yourself experiencing fear, put the fear into words, where it will become more manageable. What exactly is it that you are afraid of, and why?
5. As with self-doubt, champions conquer fear by first identifying it as an enemy they need to conquer.
6. Fear is a prison. Conquering fear wins you the freedom to fulfill your potential.
7. Conquering fear includes the willingness to step out of your comfort zone. Stepping out of your comfort zone in turn strengthens your ability to conquer fear.
8. Fear saps your energy. Conquering fear increases your energy. Increasing your energy in turn strengthens your ability to conquer fear.
9. Conquering fear empowers you with a confidence that can have an important positive influence on others, and thereby strengthen your relationship with them.
10. A "whatever it takes" mentality will help you conquer fear.
11. Taking action can stop fear in its tracks. The longer you postpone the action that will confront the fear head on, the more deeply ingrained the fear becomes.
12. Trust yourself based on what has made you successful in the past
13. Envision yourself as a champion.
14. Conquering fear includes embracing adversity and

change for the potential that lies within them.

What Is a Hero?

A hero is someone who, when faced with fear, sees beyond himself. Can anyone be a hero? Yes, because seeing beyond oneself is an act of will. It may be harder for some than for others. Some people have practiced seeing beyond themselves for a long time, so it has become natural for them. Others have grown rusty. But anyone can do it if they believe it is important.

Being a hero is one of the most rewarding opportunities of leadership, and an exciting concept to teach those you lead.

Teaching Self-Discipline

Celebrate the connection between self-discipline and self-confidence. Some managers are embarrassed to talk about self-discipline. Perhaps the idea is, "We're all adults. We don't need to talk about self-discipline. That is a topic that parents should discuss with their kids." This reluctance to address such a valuable topic is a shame, because self-discipline enhances self-confidence at any age. Self-discipline produces self-control, and self-control makes us feel more empowered – more in control of our lives and destinies.

Webster's New World Dictionary defines "discipline" as "training that develops self-control, character, or orderliness and efficiency." Self-discipline seeks to enhance this process.

In an indulgent society, some people will go so far as to regard self-discipline as a form of self-abuse, when the opposite is true. Self-discipline should be considered a form of self-love, because it is connected with the desire to improve.

Sometimes there is a tendency to shrug off self-discipline as a characteristic that not everyone was born with. However, Chandler and Richardson make an enlightening point about this:

"*If the person you lead truly understood that self-discipline is something one **uses**, not something one has, then that person could use it to accomplish virtually any goal he or she ever set*" (Chandler and Richardson 2005, p. 22).

In all aspects of life we see ways in which self-discipline boosts self-confidence. Examples include:
- Diet and exercise.
- Getting enough rest.
- Managing your schedule efficiently.
- A commitment to continuous improvement in occupations, hobbies, or relationships.
- Honoring commitments to others, even when sacrifice is involved.
- Fasting.
- Making sacrifices during religious seasons or for periodic personal rituals.

When people can master these kinds of self-discipline, they feel more prepared to handle adversity. They feel more in control of themselves, which in turn makes them feel more in control of the situations in which they are placed. Perhaps most importantly, self-discipline gives people more confidence in their ability to manage their responses to the challenges they encounter. They feel that they will be able to rise to the occasion. Perhaps this kind of confidence is the greatest blessing that self-discipline produces. It helps people feel more steady.

It also increases the confidence that others have in them. People with more self-discipline are often considered to be more reliable. Integrity is associated with self-discipline. Of course, there are many other elements that go into integrity and trustworthiness. Nevertheless, self-discipline makes a big difference in a person's reputation for steady reliability. Followers feel that they can count on someone who shows self-discipline.

People who lack self-discipline have a harder time gaining the trust of others, especially when the chips are down.

If you lead by example, and you can show your followers that you have a high degree of self-discipline, their confidence in you and in the standards of the team culture as a whole will increase. Naturally, issues of personal self-discipline outside of work that have no bearing on their professional responsibilities are beyond the scope of your leadership unless the employee is open to your guidance. However, you can certainly address any aspect of self-discipline that relates to an employee's behavior or performance on the job. Examples of this would be:

- Timely attendance. Making sure your employees are where they should be when they should be there.
- The condition in which they show up to work – their appearance, their energy level, and their state of mind.
- Their self-discipline in completing tasks on time and correctly.
- The self-discipline that is required to keep improving.
- Meeting their commitments to other team members. Here you see the connection between self-discipline and integrity in the sense of having

the self-discipline to do what they said they would when they said they would.
- The willingness to make sacrifices that are necessary to achieve goals or support other members of the team.
- Exhibiting self-control in their behavior, especially in times of stress.
- The self-discipline that is required to uphold the standards you have set for them and which their team members are upholding.

How do you coach self-discipline to your followers?

In group meetings, you can address the benefits of self-discipline in a general way. For example, you can take an approach like this:

"This year one of the goals I would like to focus on is how each of us – myself included – can use self-discipline to help us get to our next level. I've been studying the concept of self-discipline, and I've developed a whole new appreciation of what an important virtue it is, and how much of a difference it can make in getting each of us where we want to go."

You can discuss the benefits of self-discipline as we have discussed them here. If you choose this approach, be careful that you don't step on anyone's toes in a group setting. If there are people on your team who are known to struggle with this issue, such a discussion could be humiliating for them. If you have doubts about whether a public discussion of self-discipline could cause embarrassment or hurt people's feelings, it is better to err on the side of sensitivity. You always have the alternative of addressing it one on one as needed.

Keep your eyes open for examples of people whose individual self-discipline has benefited them with higher self-confidence or better results. Recognize their accomplishment. You can also give them recognition in a group setting as long as it does not cause awkwardness in the group by reflecting badly on someone else.

Conclusion

Like motivation, self-confidence comes largely from within each individual. Still, the deciding factor in many contests is a higher level of confidence which has been inspired by a leader, coach or mentor. Whether it is a military battle, an individual or team sporting event, a sales competition, a spelling bee, or an entertainment performance, the way in which a leader nurtures the confidence of his or her followers can provide the winning edge.

The kind of leadership we are talking about here can take the form of authority or it can take the form of influence. Managers, coaches and mentors all provide leadership when they are helping to build the self-confidence of another person. Helping someone else's self-confidence to blossom is one of the most valuable gifts you will ever give. Let's review the ways you can contribute to the self-confidence of your team.

1. Help them to develop a more positive self-definition.
2. Provide encouragement and reassurance, and lead them to do the same for each other. Consistent

communication is as important here as in any other aspect of motivation.
3. Make sure you project your own confidence and motivation. Your followers need to see that you have the belief in yourself and in your purpose that you are trying to inspire in them. They also need to see in you the same desire to improve every day that you are trying to instill in them.
4. Show that you have confidence in them as well as in yourself.
5. Help them to conquer self-doubt and fear using the methods described in this chapter.
6. Help followers who have never considered the benefits of self-discipline to see how it will help them become more confident and achieve the winning edge.

CHAPTER 9

TEACHING RELAXED FOCUS

We perform at our highest level, physically and mentally, when we are relaxed. Golfers hit the ball longer and straighter when their muscles are relaxed rather than tensed. Our minds work the same way. Relaxation produces mental clarity – the absence of clutter. Clarity produces focus, which in turn produces excellence. We think more quickly, clearly and intelligently when we are relaxed than when we are anxious. That is why we often have our most brilliant or inspired thoughts when we are walking through the woods, sitting on the beach, or quietly pondering a pleasant thought. We score better on tests when our minds are clear and relaxed. Achieving the highest state of relaxation in sports is called the zone. When we achieve that state in our thoughts, it's called genius.

As individuals we seek to create for ourselves a state of relaxed focus. As leaders we seek to create for our followers an environment in which a state of relaxed focus can be more easily achieved. We have already learned how to increase the motivation of your team through belief, energy, enjoyment, high standards and confidence. Achieving these breakthroughs with your team will contribute to a state of relaxed focus. In this chapter we will explore ways to help your followers spend as much of their time as possible in this most motivated and productive state. A relaxed state of focus will produce the following results:

- Clarity replaces clutter.
- Confidence replaces doubt.
- Purpose replaces ambivalence.
- Passion for excellence replaces acceptance of mediocrity.
- Joy replaces anxiety.
- Energy replaces lethargy.
- Motivation replaces complacency.

Does relaxed focus increase motivation? Absolutely. Relaxed focus gives us clarity of purpose that is single-minded and uncluttered. This clarity makes achieving our purpose seem easier. It helps us develop a laser-like focus that makes us feel unstoppable.

Now we must answer these questions: How can you as a leader use everything we have discussed throughout this book to lead your team to a state of relaxed focus? How do you get your team into the zone?

In our last chapter on self-confidence we considered how champions overcome fear. Let's take another look at champions now – not just sports champions, but champions in all walks of life. How do champions get themselves into the zone?

Thought Control

Many champions develop an extraordinary ability to control their thoughts. They begin with this question: "Do I control my thoughts or do my thoughts control me?" They assume that they must control their thoughts. Unfortunately, for many people it works the opposite. Their thoughts control them. Champions say, "How can my thoughts be in control? They are my thoughts. I own them. I create them, and then I control them." Thoughts are not like Frankenstein monsters – something we create but then can no longer control. By controlling and managing thoughts, we are better able to control and manage emotions.

One example of this kind of thought control would be how a champion handles worry. Like all of us, champions face the temptation to worry too much or overanalyze a challenge. However, they worry or analyze only as much as they feel is productive. Then they bring their productive thought process to a resolution and move on. They do not rehash unproductive thoughts over and over. When worry begins to sap their energy, they know it is time to move on.

Champions treasure mental clarity. They understand that a clearer mind produces better performance. They eliminate mental clutter. As with self-doubt and fear, they identify mental clutter as an enemy that must be conquered. They keep their heads clear by battling against thoughts that are unproductive, negative, self-limiting or self-defeating.

From time to time we need to assess the quality of our thoughts. Do we have complete control over them, or have they begun to take control of us? We need to use our thoughts as a friend, not an enemy – to unleash our potential, not to restrict it.

Thought control is making choices about what we think and how we think. Is that an oversimplification? Can we really master our own thoughts? It is largely a question of attitude and will, and champions believe it is possible. This is one of the ways champions distinguish themselves from the rest.

To control our thoughts we must appreciate that we really do have the power to choose how we respond mentally to the kinds of challenges we face. The thoughts we choose create a cumulative effect over time, and ultimately play a large role in whether we and our teams achieve mediocrity, success, or the highest level of all – long-term mastery – the level of champions.

We will talk more about how thought control actually works in our next chapter on "Teaching Mental Toughness." We need to introduce it here, however, in order to appreciate its importance in relaxed focus.

Detaching from Results

Where results are critical, use thought control to take your primary focus away from the final result while you are actually engaged in the activity. Instead of focusing on the result, allow yourself to become immersed in the moment – to become consumed in the joy of the process itself. The results will take care of themselves. Often they turn out better.

Focusing too much on results can create anxiety that depletes energy. Letting go of the results enough to enjoy the process makes you more relaxed and more confident, which improves your results, which in turn makes you even more confident and relaxed. This is another wonderful cycle.

Does this mean that being goal-oriented produces mental clutter? Not at all. The ability to set goals and stay focused on them is one of the primary ingredients in the recipe for long-term success. But when you are actually immersed in the task at hand, you must be able to detach yourself temporarily from the goals in order to absorb yourself into a relaxed, focused, joyous state – a state in which your full natural talent emerges from beneath the constraints of worry and fear. This is the clearheaded, peaceful state in which self-trust has conquered self-doubt. You are totally immersed in the love of what you are doing, and you are trusting in your ability to the point where you can trust the results to take care of themselves. In any endeavor, the mind of a champion is relaxed, yet intensely focused, motivated and stimulated. Their state of mind is positive, decisive, confident and self-trusting. It is joyful, at least for the task at hand.

Whatever the endeavor, your followers will perform their best when their minds are relaxed, absorbed and quiet – free of clutter, negativity, doubt and thoughts of failure. They are able to focus totally, clearly and peacefully, even in the midst of pressure, noise, chaos or adversity. They are in their highest and most natural state of mind. They are totally immersed in the moment and in the joy of the process.

This is the state of mind we call the zone. It is most frequently applied to sports, but the concept extends much farther. In sports the zone is a mysterious and elusive state – a simple, glorious state in which everything seems perfect and effortless. It is an almost unconscious state that athletes drift in and out of without knowing exactly how or why they got into it or slipped back out. They simply realize that when they are in the zone they are not thinking very hard. In fact, that is one of the defining characteristics of the zone: there is no mental clutter, no self-limiting thought, no self-doubt or unproductive self-criticism, no worry or fear. There is nothing interfering with their natural ability – nothing keeping them from reaching their full potential. When our minds and spirits are free from self-interference, our natural ability is an awesome force. So often we limit ourselves by underestimating our potential. Our success is limited more by our thoughts than by our abilities.

Many athletes experience the zone occasionally. Why can't they experience it all the time? Frequently it is because of self-interference. Their thoughts get in the way of their natural ability.

Yet still the zone remains so hard to explain. A golfer who is in the zone might say, "I don't know how to describe it. It's just an easy game. The fairways are 200 yards wide and the hole is 3 feet across." A basketball player who is in the zone will say, "I don't know what it is. All I can tell you is that it's a great big hoop." A hitter in baseball will say, "I could see every stitch on the ball as it was coming toward me. It seemed like slow motion."

With all the mystery of the zone, is it really possible for leaders to lead their followers in the pursuit of this elusive ideal? You will never create a situation in which every member of your team is in the zone all the time. But if you stay continually aware of how important relaxed focus is for achieving maximum performance, you can create an environment in which it is easier to achieve. Here's how.

Eliminate Fear, Clutter and Anxiety

Understanding how important relaxed focus is to motivation and performance helps you to stay vigilant about the effect your leadership is having on the relaxed focus of your followers. As you set the tone for your team culture, always keep this question in the forefront: "Will my followers be most motivated and perform at the highest level in relaxation or anxiety?"

Many leaders stumble over instilling a sense of urgency to succeed in their followers. They believe their followers underperform because they are not motivated enough, and they are not motivated enough because they do not feel urgency. These leaders often use tactics that create fear and anxiety because they believe these tactics will create more urgency. The problem with motivation by fear is that while it may create a sense of urgency, it also creates anxiety and mental clutter that lowers confidence, creates inner turmoil and reduces effectiveness. To be fair, some people do perform better under pressure, but that is because they know how. They use pressure-packed situations to their advantage by developing an inner calm while others crumble. So the pressure itself is not the motivator. They are motivated by their confidence to handle the pressure. When people say, "I love pressure," what they are really saying is, "I'm thrilled by the confidence I have developed to handle pressure." This is different from believing that you can motivate others with pressure.

If you can instill urgency without fear, you will produce a higher level of motivation and a higher state of performance. The kind of urgency that produces motivation to succeed grows more out of confidence than out of fear – more from purpose than from pressure. The kind of urgency that is created from "flight or fight" situations is something completely different, and has nothing to do with the kind of motivation we are discussing in this book. Here we are talking about the kind of motivation that you as a leader can inspire in your followers that helps them achieve long-term success.

Suppose you are considering a new career. You might imagine the new career, but you will have no urgency to pursue it until you feel confident you will succeed. As soon as you feel confident that you can succeed in the new career, and that your life will be better with the new career than with your current one, you will feel a tremendous sense of urgency to move as quickly as possible. The same is true with other major decisions, such as the decision to get married, to make a major purchase, or to enter an important competition. Fear of loss may play a part, as may fear of the consequences of staying in your current situation, but the confidence that you will be successful and that your life will improve with the new situation is what creates urgency to take action.

A motivational leader reduces fear, clutter and anxiety rather than creating it. You want your followers to be motivated by belief in themselves and in their purpose. You want them to be motivated by the vision of a positive outcome, not the fear of a negative one. The more confident they are, the more clearheaded they will be, and the closer you will come to achieving the zone for your team.

Instill an Attitude of Relaxation

Instead of an environment of fear, clutter and anxiety, create for your followers an environment of relaxation that will help them maintain a clearheaded focus on achieving excellence and fulfilling their mission. Discuss this concept with them. Tell them it is your ideal, and why you believe it is important. Explain the benefits we have discussed. We have already seen how an environment of enjoyment (Chapter Five) and an environment of high standards (Chapter Six) go hand in hand. Don't be afraid to have fun. Enjoy yourself and encourage your followers to enjoy themselves. There is nothing about relaxed focus that dilutes seriousness of purpose or a commitment to high standards.

Don't shoulder the responsibility for a relaxed, positive environment alone. Your followers need to do their part, too. Give them some responsibility for positive influence – for keeping themselves and each other pumped up. Explain to them that an atmosphere of relaxed focus is a mutual responsibility. If they are feeling negative, they need to keep it out of meetings and off the grapevine. If they feel they have a legitimate grievance, they need to come to you. They cannot be allowed to undermine the team's commitment to maintain an environment of relaxed focus. As a leader you should not create clutter, and as team members, neither should they.

Celebrate successes of individuals and of the team as a whole. *Enjoy* success, and the pursuit of it. One of your goals in relaxed focus is that your followers keep wanting to pursue their mission.

Pursuing excellence should not overcomplicate things. It should keep them as simple and easy as possible. So often the pursuit of excellence, especially through training programs, winds up intimidating employees by making their tasks seem more complicated. Of course, training is vital. Just don't forget that the purpose of training is to make tasks easier and more natural, not harder and more contrived – to increase confidence, not decrease it – to promote relaxed focus, not cluttered anxiety. Mental clutter is often caused when we focus so hard on doing everything right that we start pressing when we should be relaxing.

To stay relaxed, look for quick opportunities to restore your calm throughout the day. Create a list of positive thoughts, feelings, images and memories that you can recall during times of anxiety, frustration or discouragement. When you feel your mind being cluttered with useless worry or mental noise, stop thinking about results. Give your mind a break by retrieving your list. Or simply observe some of the more pleasing details around you: trees, birds, clouds, architecture, or a book of art that you keep in your work space. Allow your mind to become immersed in beauty and simplicity. Close your eyes, take deep breaths, and envision positive, pleasing, peaceful, beautiful things that have nothing to do with your purpose or your work. After your mind has relaxed enough to restore its energy, you can return to envisioning things more directly related to your success.

Instill Confidence That Goals Will Be Achieved

In discussing relaxed focus, we covered relaxation. Now let's talk about focus. You can create focus by defining a clear sense of purpose, explaining a plan to fulfill your purpose, and conveying a belief that you will fulfill your purpose if everyone does their part.

In addition to the larger goals to which you and your team have committed, set frequent, small goals for continuous improvement in specific skills and tasks. Make sure every member of your team commits to small steps to keep improving in some part of their process. You want each member of your team to feel as though they are getting better every day. This will keep their motivation continually revitalized.

For the larger, long-term mission of your team, make sure the mood is always about succeeding, not failing. Keep envisioning success. Act as though things will work out. So often managers inadvertently act as though things may not work out, as though they're hedging their bets against making a wrong prediction.

Make sure that no matter how steep the challenge may seem, everyone is thinking, "We will succeed. We can do this. We will do whatever it takes. Nothing will stop us, because we're unstoppable." While you are always focusing on ways to improve, the larger attitude needs to be, "Here's why we'll succeed," not, "Here's why we'll fail." The focus of continuous improvement is not on how bad we are, but how to get to the next level. Each person needs to remember what has made them successful in the past, and how to take those strengths to the next level.

When you are falling short of your goals, you want to understand why so you can make the appropriate adjustments and initiate the necessary improvements. But beware of "What's Wrong Syndrome," where everyone becomes so fixated on what's wrong that they lose their mental clarity, sense of purpose and confidence. "What's Wrong Syndrome" can quickly evolve from a search for solutions into a mentality of failure when it overcomes the positive energy of hope.

When obstacles appear to threaten the success of your mission, make sure your leadership maintains a tone of optimism: "We will overcome this." At the same time, providing the support to overcome obstacles is a way to protect the relaxed focus of your team. Leading the battle against obstacles is one of the most important functions a leader performs. It helps reduce the mental clutter of your followers when you identify obstacles that may threaten their success and seek out ways to eliminate those obstacles. This effort will not reduce you to the role of resident firefighter and problem solver. You are still the leader, and should delegate problem solving whenever possible. But for major obstacles you need to lead the way. You are, after all, the team's primary voice of hope – and of reason.

For the most severe obstacles, the message to your team is that the challenge is an opportunity to draw on their most valuable inner resources. These challenges can be a source of excitement, hope, and future pride when they are viewed as opportunities to stretch and grow and prove themselves. Success in the face of severe challenges becomes the material of their proudest stories for the rest of their lives. The confidence they derive from these experiences will last forever. You are the one who creates this vision for them.

Provide Direction

When you give your followers direction as described in Chapter Seven, you give them clarity that helps them to focus. Providing direction gives them a path to follow, explains how to follow it, and conveys your belief in their ability to follow the path to its final destination. They have a clearer sense of purpose, and a clearer understanding of how to fulfill their purpose. This mindset lies at the heart of relaxed focus.

Mental clutter can be the consequence of lack of direction. Direction provides clarity and purpose. Clarity and purpose produce focus.

Relaxed focus increases as confidence increases. As a leader you provide direction that produces confidence as well as clarity and purpose. People perform better when they believe they will succeed. Relaxed focus occurs when a sense of purpose is energized by confidence of success. Leaders help followers keep their mission clear, as well as the path they must follow to fulfill their mission.

To be fully engaged in their mission, your followers must know how to fulfill the mission, and they must believe it will succeed. That is where direction comes in. When you provide direction, provide optimism and support as well. Direction says, "This is what to do, how to do it and why to do it." Optimism with support says, "If you do it that way, I'll be at your side and together we will succeed."

Giving direction also requires you to know when to let go. As discussed in Chapter Seven, one of the goals of direction is self-sufficiency. Remember the six steps of direction:

1. Here's what to do.
2. Here's how to do it.
3. Here's why to do it that way.
4. Will you do it? When?
5. Call me after you've done it and tell me how it went.
6. Can you do it by yourself next time?

Of these six steps, the first three are about instruction, while the last three are about letting go. Once your followers know what to do, you need to let go and let them do it. This is the only way their confidence can fully blossom. Letting go is where your instruction leads to their self-sufficiency. It means that you and your followers together trust in their ability to embrace new responsibilities once they have learned how. They must believe they have the skills and ability to do it, as well as your confidence that they can do it. You provide direction not only to enhance your followers' skill, growth and self-sufficiency, but also to create relaxed focus.

When your followers are in a state of relaxed focus, they have clearheaded confidence that allows them to detach from worries about results in order to immerse themselves in the joy of the process. Training and practice help build the kind of confidence that leads to relaxed focus. Through training and practice, skills become habits, and then instincts.

Help Followers With Their Perspective

Another profound way a leader can influence is by teaching perspective. As important as it is to teach followers the skills necessary to succeed, it is even more important to teach them how to think successfully. You have already learned to think successfully. That is why you're a leader. The next step is to pass it on.

Perspective is an extraordinary gift for a leader to provide. Perspective is the point of view from which we see things – how we perceive them – how we think about the situations we confront and the people with whom we interact. We respond to people and situations based on how we view them.

Our lives are shaped largely by the way we interpret the world around us – our perspective. What your followers may need in order to handle their challenges more effectively is a different way of seeing the challenge. People often achieve their greatest breakthroughs by changing the way they perceive a challenge. Sometimes they just need to get a different point of view from someone else – someone they trust and respect. Providing perspective is one of the most valuable contributions a leader, coach or mentor can make to those they influence.

As a nation, Americans enjoy a unique quality of life largely because of George Washington's ability to provide his soldiers with the perspective they needed in order to persevere through the seemingly impossible challenge of defeating the most respected military force in the world. As if risking their lives for that foolhardy enterprise were not discouraging enough, many other factors undermined their motivation: illness, injury, hunger, harsh weather, lack of experience or skill, lack of ammunition, problems getting paid by the government for whom they were fighting, and continual desertions by their fellow soldiers. Even without these adversities, many of the soldiers doubted whether they would truly be better off with their own government than under English rule.

However, they believed in their leader, largely because he demonstrated his belief in them. His courage and perseverance inspired them. If a man of Washington's character, intelligence, credibility and dignity was willing to risk his life for the cause of freedom by riding into battle with them, it must mean that providing future generations with lives of greater dignity and opportunity was an ideal worth fighting for, no matter what the odds. Armed with new motivation that came from stronger belief in themselves and in their purpose, they would not give up until victory was theirs. They learned a new perspective for facing a situation many considered hopeless, and they learned it from their leader.

Just as Washington changed history for his country by providing a motivational change in perspective, Winston Churchill did the same for England during its darkest hour of relentless attack from Germany in World War II. British citizens found the courage and will to persevere because Churchill's perspective on courage, will and perseverance was contagious.

What does all of this have to do with relaxed focus? Mental clutter is frequently caused by having the wrong perspective, while mental clarity results from having the right perspective. As a leader you can teach your followers to see things in different, more productive ways. You can offer a new point of view that will help them respond more confidently, cope more easily, perform more successfully.

If you are leading a sales team in a tough market, they may be discouraged by their perspective of working harder and earning less than they did the year before. Guide them toward a more motivating perspective by explaining that these are the conditions in which they develop new skills, qualities and attitudes which will reward them for the rest of their lives. Help them embrace the perspective that mastering their current challenge will define them as someone who perseveres when others give up and succeeds when others fail. Success has no meaning when everyone achieves it.

Do your followers have the information they need in order to think most productively for their situation? Do they see things as they really are, and in the right proportion? Do they understand why things are the way they are? Do they understand the reasoning behind a strategy or a change? Do they see the situation from the point of view of those who will be affected? Do they see points of view beyond those which merely serve their own interests? Do they see the big picture? In the famous words of newsman Paul Harvey, do they "know the rest of the story?" Are they even interested? Or are their perspectives formed solely on the basis of their own self-serving agendas?

Leaders help their followers to see the importance of the bigger picture – to have a vision beyond themselves. They help their followers to connect the dots and understand things in a larger context so they can interpret their circumstances with greater wisdom. Your followers will say, "You made me more successful by giving me a better way to see things."

Sometimes perspective is about attitude, other times it is about perception. It might be about what to focus on and what to let go of – what you can control and what you can't – what you need to worry about and what you don't. Perspective can include understanding the context of issues where you only see or hear one part of the story – filling in the blanks. Sometimes it is about self-fulfilling prophecies. Or it could be about controlling and managing your thoughts.

Let's look at some examples of how you can teach perspective to your followers in a way that takes them closer to a state of relaxed focus.

"It's the end of the story" vs. "It's a work in progress."

When something happens that upsets us, we instinctively gravitate toward one of two interpretations of the event. We interpret it as the end of the story, or we interpret it as a work in progress. If we have a blowup with another person, we either believe that the relationship is irreparably damaged, or we feel as though the relationship will be redeemed, and may even become better than ever. If we do something that makes us look bad, we either believe we will look bad forever, or we believe we will get the opportunity to redeem ourselves and the bad incident will ultimately be forgotten or forgiven. If we fail, we either feel as though we are a failure forever, or we believe the failure will lead to future success.

You can help your followers with their perspective by reminding them that it's not the end of the story yet. Everything evolves. Bad things can become good things. Anger can become joy. We are all a work in progress, and so is the world around us. When we view events as evolving, especially when they are unpleasant, it helps us to keep our reactions under control. We are less likely to overreact. Our thoughts move to a more productive level. We can redirect them toward an attitude of, "What will it take to turn the adversity from something bad into something good?" We can think more tranquil, encouraging thoughts, such as, "It's not the end of the world," or, "This too shall pass."

Seeing challenges as positive vs. negative.

The right perspective can be our most powerful weapon in the battle against adversity. You can help followers to adjust their perspective by showing them how to embrace adversity as a challenge, a gift, an opportunity to grow, to expand their comfort zone, to break through to their next level. Help them to see challenges as stimulating – as energy sources instead of energy depleters.

Help them to see beyond the current inconvenience and discomfort – to treasure the opportunity to develop a broader range of mastery and a higher level of confidence. Encourage them to see themselves as someone who can rise to the occasion. Remind them that handling adversity is one of the most important ways to set themselves apart from the rest of the pack.

Coaching them toward a healthier perspective for adversity may also require you to provide direction for specific adjustments they must make.

Looking for good vs. looking for bad.

We see some people who consistently look for the good in bad situations, while others look for the bad in good situations. It's all a matter of perspective. One of the differences between these two approaches is this: people who look for the good are usually aware that they do it, while those who look for the bad are not aware of their tendency. That is because this difference in perspective is a matter of thought control. We have to train ourselves to look for the good in bad situations. We sometimes hear people say, "She's just naturally optimistic," or, "She has a bright outlook." This is not giving that person enough credit. A positive outlook is an act of will. It is a mental discipline. We train ourselves to do it. We discipline ourselves to see past the bad in people or situations that cause us anxiety, and we consciously seek out the good in them. This is the way we get the most out of a situation or a relationship. It is also the way we get the most out of ourselves.

"Will I succeed?" vs. "What will it take to succeed?"

In the clutterless state of relaxed focus, failure is not on the radar. Your followers may need your help in taking failure out of play. A "What will it take?" mentality is one part of a perspective for success. Help them to assume they will succeed. They just have to do what it takes. You help them find that motivation by helping them to believe in themselves and in their purpose. With these beliefs come the desire to improve – to do whatever it takes to master whatever challenge they face and achieve whatever goal they pursue. Through your leadership they find the motivation to succeed. Through your direction they learn the way to succeed. You can help nurture the "whatever it takes" mentality by helping them keep their self-definitions on track, their vision of success and its rewards clear, and their trust in you from wavering. The next two perspectives we will discuss relate to this one.

Assuming things will work vs. won't.

Help your followers appreciate the value of self-fulfilling prophecies. Assume they will succeed and not fail – that they will win and not lose. If they are in sales, assume that they will make a sale, not that they won't. Help them focus on why people do buy their product, not why they don't.

This is another aspect of thought control. There is simply no reason to assume failure. It doesn't matter if the assumption of success is accurate. Some people don't assume success because they are more afraid of being wrong than of failing. But in this case it's not about being correct. It's about being successful. They will be more successful if they pursue their mission as though they will succeed. In a state of relaxed focus, people assume they will succeed. They perform at a higher level because they are performing with more belief in themselves and in their purpose. They are more energized and more clearheaded.

If you are introducing a new strategy, make sure your followers understand the reasoning and purpose behind the strategy. If they don't, they might assume the new strategy will be less successful than the old one. Why would they assume this? Simply because they understand the old strategy better. We have a higher sense of belief in that which we understand. We are more comfortable with it. You can lead them to that same sense of belief and comfort in a new strategy. If they trust you, they will be more open to your new ideas because they believe that you have their best interests at heart.

Obstacles won't stop you vs. will stop you.

Our last two perspectives lead into this one. Obstacles exist to challenge us, not to prevent us from succeeding. They provide us with opportunities to learn and stretch and grow. Overcoming them gives us the confidence we need to rise to the next level. Teach your followers that obstacles may challenge them, but won't stop them. Help them to understand that situations which challenge them offer greater rewards than those which don't. Teach the perspective to welcome challenges as a gift.

Assuming that change is good vs. bad.

The same principle applies to change. Many people don't like change because it pushes them outside their comfort zone. But that is how our comfort zone grows. Change forces people to learn how to adapt. Leaders play a huge role in helping their followers to adapt – they lead the team to adapt to new conditions.

Change brings the idea of self-fulfilling prophecies back into play. If you believe change is bad, you will increase the likelihood that it will be bad for you. So why not choose to believe it is good, and position yourself to take advantage of the change by showing a superior ability to adapt. Once you have taught your followers a "What will it take?" mentality, they will be able to apply it here: "What will it take to make this change succeed?"

Your followers will be more confident and focused if they believe the change will benefit them. Sometimes they need a more long-term perspective in order to embrace the change.

Seeing difficult customers as an exciting challenge, not as a nuisance.

If you lead in a profession where customers provide challenges, teach your followers how to embrace these challenges with positive energy. The key to handling difficult customers is to maintain the vision of a happy ending. Teach your followers to say to themselves:

"This customer may be a real jerk, but soon they won't be a jerk any more. I can turn this situation around, and it won't take long. The way I will do it is to relax, maintain the customer's dignity, show that I like them, and show that I am committed to achieving a fair resolution to their concerns. I am a good communicator. I will give them unconditional love. Soon they will have no choice but to like me. Then they will become easier to work with."

The same is true with unmotivated customers. This is especially true in sales. Great salespeople say to themselves:

"This customer is unmotivated, but that's what I'm here for. Soon they will feel comfortable with me. After that they will begin to feel motivated. Once they are motivated they will begin to feel urgency. Before they leave they will be a delighted customer. I can do that, because that's what I do."

To handle difficult customers, replace the perspective of the customer as a nuisance or an enemy with the perspective that the customer will be a joy and a friend in the future.

Seeing beyond yourself.

Hopefully one of the reasons you attained a role of leadership is that you were recognized as a person who could see beyond yourself. You have developed the ability to see yourself and your needs in a larger context that also includes the needs of others. You see a bigger picture. You connect the dots. Recall how you reached that level of thinking. You will need to teach this perspective to some of your followers. Many people do not look beyond themselves because they are afraid to. Others simply don't know how. Either way, you can help them to change this perspective. You can also explain the need to change it.

Help your followers to understand the bigger picture. Help them to see that they are pieces of a larger puzzle and, when necessary, to see how the pieces of this puzzle fit together. Remind them of the importance of fairness to others as well as themselves. Sometimes a situation cannot be totally fair. Sometimes it can only be equally unfair to everyone. Everyone may need to give a little in order to gain in return. But isn't that the way it's supposed to be?

Challenge your followers to think about fairness without using any first-person pronouns. Everyone thinks that a situation is unfair to them at some point. But if it is equally unfair to everyone else, then at least it's a level playing field. Isn't that what they are really asking for? Or are they really just asking for preferential treatment which they are trying to disguise as fairness? People frequently believe that they deserve preferential treatment because they have earned it. They often need an outside perspective in order to view the situation more objectively. They may also need to learn the perspective that fairness needs time to play out.

Recognize the people on your team who master the perspective of seeing beyond themselves.

Reinforce to your team the vital truth that we are at our best and strongest when we are thinking beyond ourselves. This unselfish state enhances relaxed focus.

Back to thought control.

As your followers become more aware of the concept of relaxed focus, and how important the right perspective is in achieving success, guide them to become more aware of the need to continually assess the quality of their thoughts. As they realize that they have the ability and responsibility to manage the quality of their thoughts, they can begin to ask themselves questions like:

1. Are my thoughts productive?
2. Am I fixating on something which will serve no positive purpose?
3. Am I subjecting myself to negative self-talk?
4. Am I succumbing to fear or self-doubt?
5. Am I creating a negative self-definition?
6. Am I overcomplicating things?
7. Am I getting consumed in "What's wrong syndrome?"
8. Am I sapping my own energy by assuming negative results when I could be giving myself energy by assuming positive ones?
9. Am I allowing clutter into my mind which clouds the clarity I need for relaxed focus?

Teaching perspective will help your team win the battle of clarity vs. clutter and achieve relaxed focus. Teaching relaxed focus will take your team to a higher level of performance. It will also take them to a higher level of motivation by increasing their joy of the process they pursue in order to achieve their mission, and by eliminating the negative forces which threaten their motivation.

An understanding of relaxed focus sets the stage for the final frontier we will explore in the world of motivation – mental toughness.

Chapter 10

TEACHING MENTAL TOUGHNESS

Mental toughness is a distinguishing trait of champions in many professions, from sports to business to politics to art. Mental toughness enhances such adventurous undertakings as exploration and invention. It is not ruthless, cynical, mean-spirited, or a coldly indifferent to the world. It is not about "looking out for Number One" at all costs. In fact, it is quite the opposite.

We saved this chapter for last because it is the culmination of everything discussed throughout this book. We will revisit some earlier ideas to see how they apply to mental toughness, and how mental toughness applies to motivation. Mental toughness takes motivation to a deeper level. It has its roots in belief in self and purpose, and in the desire to improve every day. It is not fear-driven or insecure. It is the desire to do whatever it takes. But it is more.

Mental toughness is a way of thinking, and anyone can do it. Your followers can develop mental toughness just as surely as they develop physical fitness. It grows out of the kind of mental disciplines we have discussed in previous chapters. It includes choosing and managing the right thought process. If you and your team focus on mental toughness, you will develop it.

Developing mental toughness begins with recognizing what it is, the difference it can make between success and failure, and how much control you have over it. Some people have a hard time developing mental toughness simply because they have not thought about it. Like physical fitness, mental toughness begins when you appreciate its importance, and then develops through self-discipline, practice, and a willingness to step out of your comfort zone in order to take your success to the next level.

Mental toughness positions your followers for a higher level of motivation. As a leader, you want to teach mental toughness to your followers, and you want to create an environment in which it can flourish. You want a team that is defined in part by its mental toughness. Express to your team that it is an ideal you want to strive for – that it is your desire for the team as a whole and for every individual on the team.

Now let's see how you can lead them toward this ideal. We will begin by seeing how the ideas we discussed about thought control can serve as a foundation for mental toughness.

Thought Control

People who are mentally tough take responsibility for the quality of their thoughts. Thought control has been a recurring theme throughout this book. We have seen its importance in a variety of areas that are critical to motivation:

- Belief
- Energy
- Enjoyment
- Self-confidence (including the ability to overcome fear and self-doubt)
- Relaxed focus

Now let's look at another dimension of thought control that produces mental toughness.

Focus on What You Can Control

One of the defining characteristics of mental toughness is the ability to *detach yourself from things you cannot control.* This enables you to redirect your energy and your focus more productively on those things you can control. If you are stuck in traffic, you cannot control the speed at which you choose to drive, but you can control how you use the time the slowdown is causing you to "waste." If you are selling in a tough market, you cannot control the market conditions, but you can give a first-rate presentation to the next customer you encounter. If you are being slandered, you cannot control what is being said about you, but you can control the dignity of your demeanor as you endure the controversy.

Many people are unable to fulfill their potential because their energy is sapped by fixating on factors beyond their control. Champions accept the fact that we are all affected by things beyond our control. They see the potential for gaining a competitive advantage by setting aside those factors they cannot control in order to focus more willfully on areas where they can make a difference. This *decision* of thought control enhances their mental clarity and intensity for the task at hand.

Explain this principle to your followers. It is another case where the awareness of the principle is the springboard to mastering it. Make your followers aware that anyone can do this. It is simply a mental discipline. If they become aware when they are fixating on issues they can't control, they can switch their focus. They may not be able to prevent themselves from beginning to focus on things they cannot control, but if they can catch themselves in the act and stop, that is good enough. At that point they can redirect their thoughts in order to focus more clearly, intensely and productively on those things they can control. This adjustment will have an enormous impact on their level of success, their self-confidence and their mental toughness.

This idea leads us to another form of mental discipline – the ability to compartmentalize your thoughts.

Compartmentalization

Mental toughness doesn't mean that you can't enjoy life, that you can't stop and smell the roses along the way. Mental toughness is not the same as constant intensity. It is something you draw upon when there is a need. In fact, joy and relaxation are essential ingredients in mental toughness. People who are mentally tough have the confidence to balance relaxation with intensity. They are able to hold on when they need to, and also to let go when they need to.

One element of mental toughness is the ability to *compartmentalize* – such as creating a compartment in your mind for adversity that keeps it from spoiling everything else. The adversity, after all, is not your whole life, even though it may seem to be for awhile. It is only one of many parts of a much larger picture. Managing distractions and maintaining focus is an important part of mental toughness.

We discussed how to achieve relaxed focus in our last chapter. Here is another way to maintain focus and clarity in the face of adversity and distraction:

Imagine that your mind is made up of a series of cylinders that you can slide in and out of your mind at will. Each cylinder contains a different issue, and you have control over opening and closing those cylinders. All of the cylinders remain shut except the one you choose to open. Each time you open a cylinder you deal with that issue the best way you can in the time available. Then you put that issue back into its cylinder and open another one. You never open more than one cylinder at a time, so no situation can ever spill over into the other cylinders. The key to this process is realizing that you control the cylinders. Mentally tough champions have this ability to compartmentalize in order to maintain mental clarity for the challenge at hand, even in the face of an adversity that might immobilize someone else.

We have talked about handling various kinds of adversity in previous chapters. Now let's revisit adversity one last time as it applies to mental toughness.

Embracing Adversity

Embracing adversity and persevering through it builds your mental toughness. Cherish this evolution in your mental toughness even as it is occurring. Never lose sight of the positive value of adversity. As miserable as it may be while you are enduring it, if you can embrace it as a gift, an opportunity, and a step along the path to future success, you will increase your mental toughness. Step outside of your difficult situation in order to see that it is temporary, and that it is an opportunity to develop your mental and emotional stamina so that future challenges will be easier. Adversity is the time when new strengths develop.

Weathering our occasional storms requires a healthy perspective of big-picture, long-term thinking that places our challenges and adversities into the larger context of ultimate success.

Adversity can become consuming. Success in handling adversity begins by viewing it as something that everyone confronts at some point. Adversity is not a fluke, but a universal experience. Champions see adversity as a level playing field where they gain an advantage. They do not view adversity as an injustice, but as an opportunity to prove that they are champions.

In normal situations champions win by excelling. Adversity provides an opportunity for champions to win by staying afloat while others sink. This is one reason some champions seem to thrive on adversity. They find excitement in an opportunity to weather a challenge or setback in order to eventually separate themselves from the pack. They become inspired by the opportunity to persevere when others would give up, to hang on when others would let go. They see past the failure and pain of the setback to envision the success and joy that will follow.

When you are faced with adversity, begin by envisioning the end of the adversity, with you triumphant.

Do not become consumed with feelings that the situation is unfair. This is one downfall of non-champions. Anger and negativity caused by the injustice of adversity can become an anchor that pulls many people down, while the champion is using the same adversity as a springboard for motivation, determination and, eventually, success over the long term. While average people are dragged down by jealousy over the good fortune of others, champions are creating future good fortune of their own.

Perseverance

We have talked about a "What will it take?" mentality – a single-minded focus on achieving an objective – an unshakable, unstoppable sense of purpose. This mentality also includes perseverance – a fierce determination not to give up when others would. Champions with a "whatever it takes" mentality believe that *choosing* to overcome fear or frustration leads to winning. They believe that if you persevere, things will work out. Perseverance is one of the highest forms of mental toughness.

A "whatever it takes" mentality is a "no excuses" mentality. For many people an excuse for not achieving a result is as good as the result itself. Not the champion. The champion is hungry for achievement, and excuses don't satisfy that hunger.

Some people are "starters" while others are "finishers." Those with a "whatever it takes" mentality are both. They take the initiative to start things that others are unwilling to start, and then they finish them. They persevere when others would give up. They do things that others are unwilling to do in order to get the job done. They are willing to make sacrifices while others believe that making the sacrifice is unfair. A "whatever it takes" mentality realizes that being a champion is as much about the *will* as it is about natural ability.

There are some days when everything seems hard. You feel as though you're grinding just to break even. Yet during these times just hanging in there may turn out to be your winning edge, if those around you are dragged down and you are not. A tough stretch is only one chapter in a book with many other exciting chapters. Wait for the tide to turn, or for your second wind to kick in. It always does. If you maintain your clarity, and stay loose but focused, you will get through this challenge in a way that will keep you fresh and strong for the next one.

In some contests the winner is the person with the most points at the end. In others, the winner is the one who is still standing at the end. Often the difference is not talent or skill, but mental toughness.

Victory over opponents makes someone a winner. Victory over adversity makes them a champion. Conquering adversity is one of the defining characteristics of a champion.

The Correct Balance of Patience and Impatience

Challenges often take time to resolve. They may evolve through a series of stages, and some of these stages can be difficult. You may have to go through tough times in order to reach the good times. Things may appear confusing before they finally make sense. Things sometimes have to fall apart in order to come back together in a better way than you ever imagined. These kinds of ups and downs are more normal than we may realize when we are in the middle of them. Dealing with evolving situations requires patience – the kind of patience we associate with perseverance. However, there are also those times when you have to be impatient enough to break through and make things happen. Mental toughness includes the ability to balance patience with impatience in order to adapt correctly to the variety of challenges you will face.

You need the patience to give a situation the time it needs in order to evolve. You have to persevere during that time with a "whatever it takes" mentality. You may have to accomplish your objectives in increments in order for the desired result to be achieved. You may also have to be patient in the sense of realizing that your final result may be different from what you had envisioned. However, a new direction may offer a greater opportunity than the direction you originally envisioned.

However, being patient with evolving challenges is not the same as being a victim of them. As we said earlier, mental toughness combines the ability to detach yourself from things you cannot control in order to cope with them better, and redirect your energy more productively to those things you can control. With things you cannot control, you may need to let go and allow them to follow their course. But they can follow their course more advantageously for you when you focus your energy on things you can control. This is where impatience comes into play.

There are times when your patience needs to run out in order for you and your team to move forward. You may need to lose patience with your situation, with another individual, with your team as a whole, or with yourself. You realize that the time has finally come to say:

- "It's time to resolve this. The solution cannot be postponed any longer." (Or, "We need to set a deadline for when we will resolve this, and we need to do whatever it takes to meet that deadline.")
- "Failure is not an option."
- "I need for you to honor the commitment you made."
- "I need the answers now that only you can supply."

- "The time for excuses has run out."
- "It's time to make the best decision we can and move forward. We can't stand still any longer."

Adaptability and Flexibility

Just as adversity offers exciting opportunities, so does uncertainty. Like the fear of change, the fear of uncertainty is another enemy you must conquer in order to achieve your full potential. Mental toughness involves developing *flexibility* and *adaptability*. The ability and willingness to adapt and be flexible is another distinguishing characteristic of champions. They realize that if they can adapt to a wider variety of situations more quickly and easily than other people, they will come out on top in the long run. This is why champions are more comfortable with change than others.

You will need to adapt to situations you cannot control in order to maximize the opportunities you can control. Assume change will work to your benefit, and you will be better equipped to take advantage of the opportunities the change provides. Adaptability and perseverance go hand in hand. While it is necessary to adapt to changes in your circumstances, stay focused and committed to accomplishing your purpose.

Embrace change as an opportunity to establish one more competitive advantage while others are floundering in fear, doubt, cynicism and other negative reactions to the uncertainty of change. There are a variety of ways for things to work out well. Stay focused on these possibilities, and not the variety of ways that things might not work out. Adversity and change are opportunities for adaptable people to keep growing while others reach their plateau.

Adaptability is not a talent. It is an attitude we develop through our will. It requires:
- Open-mindedness
- Willingness to embrace new adventures
- The kind of courage that grows out of self-trust

Be Willing To Take Your Medicine

When you fail or blunder, be willing to accept responsibility and consequences. Then get back up and keep going. Everyone has setbacks. Champions display the mental toughness to keep going when others give up, and they bounce back from setbacks more quickly. They see the setback as a growth step. They view everything as a gift, realizing that they may not understand why a setback is a gift until later. They don't fret over the unfairness of the setback, because they realize how destructive such attitudes can be. They believe that if they take their medicine, the medicine will eventually make them better.

Now let's look at several other dimensions of mental toughness.

Self-Confidence

We explored self-confidence in detail in Chapter Eight. Let's consider its importance in mental toughness.

People with mental toughness are motivated. They have a strong belief in themselves and their purpose, and they have a desire to improve every day. They see themselves in terms of positive self-definitions, and avoid negative ones. They identify negative self-talk and replace it with positive self-talk. They master self-discipline, because they understand its value. What else can you do to make sure your self-confidence radiates mental toughness?

Identify negative thoughts such as self-doubt and fear as enemies that must be conquered in order for you to keep moving forward. Whenever you are pursuing a noble cause, these enemies will try to discourage you. Fear achieves its victory when it persuades you to give up by attacking your self-confidence and hope. We sometimes succumb to fear because we don't identify it as an enemy as quickly as we should.

Mental toughness includes the ability to step outside of yourself and objectively decide upon the best course of action without fear of, "What will become of me if it all goes wrong?" Sometimes you need to take self-interest out of the equation in order to do what is right. Don't focus on what is happening to you. Focus on what you can contribute. It will take your state of mind to a higher level.

Don't be afraid to take a few lumps. Champions take them all the time. They know when to take self-interest out of play because something greater than self-interest is hanging in the balance.

We discussed confrontation in Chapter Six. The point we want to reiterate here is its value as a component of mental toughness. Mentally tough champions view confrontation as an opportunity to achieve resolution. They have the ability to take consequences to themselves out of the equation when they need to. You may find yourself in a situation where you need to defend a principle in which you believe. You may incur a risk to yourself in defending your principle. Even in this situation you make every effort to defend the dignity of your opponent. This is the kind of mental toughness that provides satisfaction from confrontation.

The Joy of Competition

People who are mentally tough love to compete. But they love it in a wholesome way. Sometimes calling a person competitive implies that they only want to win. It is a nice way of calling them poor losers. This has nothing to do with mental toughness. People who are mentally tough love to compete whether they win or lose.

The love of competition is different than the love of winning. For mentally tough competitors, the joy of competing outweighs even the joy of winning. Of course they want to win. They love to win. But they love to compete even if they don't win. They embrace losing as an opportunity to improve.

In competition, mental toughness enables people to compete in a spirit of respect for their opponents. When people cannot compete respectfully, it means that their attitude toward competition is driven by fear. As a leader, you can encourage healthy competition as a way to develop the mental toughness of your team.

The Ability to Handle Criticism

Like taking your medicine, taking criticism is something few people enjoy. However, it can be viewed as either an injustice or an opportunity for growth. Champions use their mental toughness to benefit from criticism. Even when they feel that the criticism is unfounded, they look for the smallest kernel of validity in order to improve themselves for future victories. They embrace criticism as an opportunity to improve. They are not defensive, because defensiveness is driven by insecurity. They don't dwell on whether the critic has the right to criticize, or whether others are more deserving of the criticism. Champions look for opportunities to display courage in the face of any kind of adversity or frustration, including criticism. True motivation involves the desire to improve every day.

Empathy and Mental Toughness

Empathy is certainly a virtue. The ability to see things from the point of view of others will increase your success. However, mental toughness means you cannot become inappropriately empathetic (or sympathetic) in ways that put your mission at risk. It is important to be compassionate, to be sensitive to the needs of others, to take a detour from your plan for someone in need. However, mentally tough champions allow themselves to empathize with the feelings of others without allowing the empathy to deter them from fulfilling their purpose, or doing what they believe is right.

Mental toughness means being willing to make tough decisions. Sometimes empathy makes those decisions even tougher. Make sure your decisions are based on sound principles, and not merely on the path of least resistance. Suppose you work in a business that serves customers. You have an employee who repeatedly takes the customers' side against your company because his "empathy" for customers makes him unwilling to hold them accountable for honoring their responsibilities. Is this true empathy, or is it merely a fear of confrontation? The employee needs to hold his customers as accountable for their responsibilities as they hold him.

Tough love is another example of the balance of compassion with mental toughness. When are you showing true compassion, and when are you simply being an enabler? Beware of those times when your compassion can become a liability to yourself and to others. There are certainly times when the right thing to do is to set aside your mission for the well-being of another person. But you cannot get dragged down by someone whose unwillingness to fulfill their responsibilities puts at risk those who are depending on you to fulfill yours. You always want to help each member of your team become more successful, especially when they're down. At the same time, you cannot allow empathy, sympathy or compassion to undermine the spirit of accountability that is so important to motivation.

Feeling empathy for others can sometimes force us to face tough decisions. When an employee has a good heart, you want to forgive him for not upholding a standard, when you would feel less forgiving of a more selfish employee. Perhaps his good-heartedness truly has earned extra time and effort from you in coaching and counseling him to rise to the team standard. However, if he remains unable or unwilling to meet the standard, and you take no action because you empathize with his struggle ("after all, no one is perfect"), you place the standard at risk, along with the morale of your team.

As hard as it may seem to make these decisions, the consequences of not making them are worse. Fortunately, the solution to these dilemmas often lies squarely in the realm of integrity. Balancing integrity with empathy will help you make the tough decisions with the confidence and conviction that your decision is based on sound principles. So let's look at integrity – an appropriate way to conclude our exploration into the world of mental toughness, and of motivation.

Integrity

Integrity can be an energizing and strengthening force behind mental toughness. While mental toughness can exist in the absence of integrity, integrity takes mental toughness to a higher level. When you believe in the integrity of your mission and purpose, you pursue it with the passion and energy that characterize mental toughness. You are also aware of the superior reputation you build in the process.

Mental toughness in its highest form includes maintaining your integrity and defending your principles, no matter how hard it may seem. You are serving a purpose greater than yourself. Integrity often requires sacrifice. Sometimes you must even take self-interest entirely out of the equation in order to do what is right. Mental toughness is believing that if you defend a valid principle, even at your own risk, you will become stronger, develop a better reputation, and the results will take care of themselves. Mental toughness involves a commitment to defend your standards and maintain dignity in all situations. You will stand taller and be more fearless when you trust that high standards will prevail. This attitude inspires you with confidence and energy that transmits to others.

Teaching mental toughness to your followers in this way can help them not only to appreciate its value, but also to see that it is within their reach. Mental toughness is not an elusive gift available only to a chosen view. It is a wonderful virtue for achieving a successful and fulfilling life, and it is available to everyone.

Conclusion

With mental toughness we complete our journey through the world of motivational leadership. The purpose of this book has been to explore what it takes to be a motivating leader – how to think like a motivating leader, and how to put those thoughts into action. The principles, thoughts and techniques discussed throughout this book will help you achieve the following goals of motivational leadership:

1. Increase your followers' belief in themselves and in their purpose.
2. Increase their desire to keep improving.
3. Provide the kind of external motivation that nurtures their internal motivation. (To motivate them, and to teach them how to motivate themselves.)
4. Increase their feelings of confidence, joy, energy, hope and self-sufficiency.
5. Help them to keep improving their self-definitions.
6. Inspire a commitment to higher standards.
7. Help them to develop more empowered perspectives.
8. Develop a pattern of consistent communication that not only conveys information, but also achieves resolution.
9. Help them to conquer fear.
10. Improve performance by creating conditions for relaxed focus.
11. Help them develop to mental toughness.
12. Develop a reputation as a leader that people want to follow.

Motivation From the Heart

When your leadership inspires a passion in your followers to be the best they can be, you are demonstrating motivation from the heart – the highest and most fulfilling form of motivational leadership.

BIBLIOGRAPHY

Bell, Chip R. *Managers as Mentors.* San Francisco: Berrett-Koehler Publishers, 2002.

Bruce, Ann and James S. Pepitone. *Motivating Employees.* New York: McGraw-Hill, 1999.

Chandler, Steve and Scott Richardson. *100 Ways to Motivate Others.* Franklin Lakes, NJ: Career Press, 2005.

Loehr, Jim and Tony Schwartz. *The Power of Full Engagement.* New York: Free Press (A Division of Simon & Schuster, Inc.), 2003.

Robbins, Anthony. *Unlimited Power.* New York: Free Press (A Division of Simon & Schuster, Inc.), 1986.

ABOUT THE AUTHORS

After a successful career in sales and management in the home building industry, **Richard Tiller** formed Tiller Marketing Services in 1991 to serve home builders as a coach, trainer and motivator for salespeople and managers. In addition to his seminars and personal coaching, he has provided guidance and motivation across the United States through his books and newsletters on sales, leadership, motivation and fulfillment. His website is www.richardtiller.com.

Paul Renker's success as a salesperson led to an outstanding career as vice president of sales for a major national home builder. There he established a reputation for providing the kind of leadership that motivates and produces excellent results in all market conditions. His success as a leader has been credited largely to his ability to motivate those he leads to a high level of belief in themselves and in their purpose, and by living the principles of leadership which are taught in this book.

To order this book or learn about other available materials, see our website at www.richardtiller.com.